Simon's book is a power!  God can bring a lost sou a rock'. The mire was, in Jordan war zone which also seeking to escape fro ing his life. However, God ...au vuici ideas.

Simon's dramatic escape from the minefield and subsequent events took him first to prison, and eventually to finding Jesus' love and forgiveness in a supportive church.

Simon had been in prison for dealing drugs, but now he works, alongside his wife, for the Kairos Prison Ministry, visiting prisons and churches, telling his story and 'dealing' hope not drugs.

His book is an eloquent and well-written account of this upward journey. It could help signpost addicts, worried parents, prisoners and prison chaplains to the truth that lasting healing for the lost and the broken can be found in the 'Higher Power' that has a name, and that name is Jesus.

Richard Stephens, chair of Kairos

A Second Chance takes you on a rollercoaster of a ride. Simon is a man with nine lives; his story demonstrates that no matter how lost we become, God has a plan to deliver and restore us.

Ian McDowall, founder of Tough Talk

Simon's journey out of addiction is intriguing and it demonstrates that, in the process of recovery, there is no 'one size fits all'. An interesting and insightful read, with encouragement and hope for anyone in addiction looking for a different path.

Barry Woodward, author of Once an Addict *and CEO of Proclaim Trust*

Simon's story is a reminder that nobody is out of the reach of God's love to forgive and power to restore a broken life. That's the gospel in a nutshell. What I found refreshing is that Simon doesn't paint a bed-of-roses picture of his discipleship journey but is honest about his struggles. This book will no doubt touch many lives.

Rod Williams, founder of Real Deal Ministries

A wild ride from start to finish, Simon's story is living proof that everyone, no matter their past, can have a new life, purpose and destiny.

Carl Beech, CEO of Edge Ministries, president of Christian Vision for Men

A Second Chance

Breaking free from the cycle of addiction and bad choices

Simon Williams

Authentic

First published 2023 by Authentic Media Limited,
PO Box 6326, Bletchley, Milton Keynes, MK1 9GG.
authenticmedia.co.uk

British Library Cataloguing in Publication Data
A catalogue record for this book is available from the British Library.
ISBN: 978-1-78893-320-9
978-1-78893-321-6 (e-book)

Cover design by Claire Marshall
Printed and bound by CPI Group (UK) Ltd, Croydon, CR0 4YY

Some names have been changed to protect the privacy of individuals.

Contents

Foreword

The prologue of this book is well-written and captivating. It is an indication of the unfolding drama of the amazing story of Simon Williams' life, as he lurched from one hair-raising scheme to another, fuelled so often with drug and alcohol parties. If you pick this book up you will find it hard to put down, as you cannot help but get drawn into the account of this man's broken life, until it is transformed by the grace of God.

I have known Simon and his wife Suzanne for almost twenty years and can vouch for their integrity and honesty as they open their hearts and share with us the painful struggles they both went through. They have been committed and active members of our church so I know them well.

Simon takes us through his early years which were far from easy as his father joined the Merchant Navy and saw more of the sea than his family. Violent clashes between his parents because of his dad's sessions of drinking alcohol had a detrimental effect on his early development as a child. Simon became restless and had little meaning or purpose to his life; cannabis soon became his comfort blanket and the only way of blotting out the pain.

As you read the book you will find it hard to believe the risks Simon and his friends took and the dangerous situations they found themselves in. Their travels and parties took them to Germany, Athens, Cyprus, Egypt, Thailand and Israel, to mention a few countries.

Yet through it all Simon began to feel that God was watching over him and causing unusual things to happen. He went to India to look into the teaching of Buddhism. He listened to talks by the Dalai Lama but found he couldn't engage with his mystical messages. After a few girlfriends he met Suzanne, who stayed with him in spite of his irrational behaviour. They had three children but their relationship at times hit rock bottom because Simon couldn't break free from his addictions. The book concludes with the journey Simon made in committing his life to God and seeking deliverance from the demons of addiction and bad choices.

No addict lives in isolation as there are family members who suffer as well. The pain that was inflicted on Simon's mother, Cynthia, and his wife, Suzanne, as a result of his behaviour was hard for them to bear. Both of them are now committed Christians and, having experienced God's healing grace, now live in a loving relationship together.

Simon is a transformed character, though he would be the first to admit that he is still a work in progress. He and Suzanne are now on the leadership team of his home church where they lead a Grow Group. Simon also leads a Freedom in Christ course, as well as working in one of our prisons under the banner of Kairos Prison Ministry, an international group that seeks to address the spiritual needs of men in prison, a place that Simon visited on more than one occasion. Simon's transformation is summed up in these words: 'If anyone is in Christ, he is a new creation. The old has passed away; behold, the new has come' (2 Cor. 5:17, ESV).

Be sure to read this book and to pass it on.

This book has great value in three areas:

1. It will encourage and inspire Christians as they learn again of God's patience and grace to transform a broken person's life.
2. It will bring hope to parents who have a son or daughter trapped in addiction to believe that God can transform them as he has Simon.
3. It will bring expectation to other drug and alcohol addicts as they realize there is a way out of their despair and darkness into the light and freedom of knowing God's deliverance.

Foreword by Victor Jack, evangelist and Bible teacher, initiator of Sizewell Hall Christian Conference and Camping Centre as well as chairman of the Garden Tomb in Jerusalem for some twelve years.

I would like to dedicate this book to my children.

Acknowledgements

I would first and foremost like to thank my Lord and Saviour, Jesus Christ, for giving me not just a second chance but many chances.

I also want to thank my mum for putting up with me during my turbulent years and for being a best friend throughout my lifetime, and also a heavenly thanks to my dad, who is now with our Lord, for providing well for our family. Thank you, too, so much to my wonderful wife, Suzanne, who has stuck with me through thick and thin and for holding our family together during some very tough years.

This book would probably not have got finished if my great friend, Ann Coleman, had not spent so many hours editing and fine-tuning this book so a special thanks to her and to her husband, Mike. Without their help and counsel and Christian friendship, I might not have been here at all to tell this story.

I have had much Christian support and prayer from some very good friends and from my local church over the years, so many thanks to all who have been and are part of my journey.

Prologue

Pain shot through the length of my body as his kick connected with my ribs, while the cords binding my hands cut any blood supply to them, turning them blue. From a corner of the thick, oppressive blindfold, I could see just enough to identify my friends as they were subject to the same treatment and mercilessly tossed into the vehicle beside me.

At least we were still together, trussed up and helpless. Alarmingly, we were surrounded by a band of highly excitable Bedouin Arabs, all toting an array of weapons – and all of them pointed at us! Their hysterical shouts and welter of bad breath smothered our groans, as our captors hurled insults at us.

Despite aching in every quarter, my brain fog was slowly lifting and clearing. I was stone-cold sober now. And we were in one hell of a mess.

I'd survived plenty of scrapes in my time during my civilian life and in the army. Authority was there to be challenged, I believed; boundaries should be pushed. But this was altogether different. This time we really were in a life-or-death situation – one I felt in that moment of remorse was chiefly down to me.

How did our small party of five become captive to an angry Arab mob? This was not how I had planned the day. This was supposed to be a birthday celebration, I reminded myself. Where and how had it all gone so horribly wrong?

But this wasn't the time to reason things out. An engine was switched on, the clutch engaged, and the ancient lorry roared into the night. The jolting was agonizing especially now as the unwelcome kicks were taking their toll.

From my limited view, all I could see was desert and more desert. Where were we going? Were they aiming to shoot us in this no man's land? Surely it couldn't end like this. We were too young to die, none of us had yet seen our thirtieth birthdays. No one knew where we were, so how on earth would they find out our fate?

If only I had thought this through. If only I had made different plans or perhaps cut down on the beers. If only, if only . . . But now it was too late.

1

The Early Years

From the start, my life has always felt like one big challenge. From calm beginnings, I emerged very much the product of parental disharmony, marked by the semi-nomadic life I lived as a child. My dad, John, joined the Merchant Navy at 17 years old and saw more of the ocean than dry land in his lifetime. I have often wondered if that adventurous spirit was passed directly down to me.

A child of the sixties, I was born in Chester, where my dad had temporarily settled for a brief spell as a police officer. His change of direction was to appease my mum, Cynthia. Although knowingly marrying a naval man, Cynthia was finding life far from plain sailing due to his long absences, often for months at a time.

I was a winter baby, born so suddenly that no medical help reached Mum in time. So I was delivered by my grandmother, Edna. That one act would bind me, in some strange way, to my grandmother for many years to come.

Grandmother Edna, who we called Gan, was a frequent presence in the family home as I grew up. She was a force to be reckoned with, due to her dominant personality. Even Mum, the soul of patience, found her mother hard to get along with. But Gan was also one big-hearted woman, who was always around when we needed help.

Sadly, my enduring memory of Gan was her frightening way of calling me to order when I got out of hand one day. She wrapped her arms tightly around me and pressed me hard to her body until, almost breathless, I calmed down. It was a terrifying, oppressive sensation, one that haunted me for years. Apart from being deeply unpleasant, there was almost a latent sexual element to it. To this day, I can't describe my feelings for Gan. However, I could never have imagined back then that, years into the future, I would need professional help to break the chain of emotions that haunted me when I thought about her.

Those early years in Chester were relatively calm and settled. But nothing in my life stays calm for long. My older brother, Andrew, was quieter and more studious than I was. He was well able to deal with the turmoil to come, by withdrawing into his own private world. Despite all the upheavals, he would go on to public school and eventually follow in Dad's footsteps. We enjoyed a typical brotherly relationship, laced with plenty of fights and fall-outs. But I didn't know him well and to this day I don't know how Andrew felt about his dad. As for me, it's fair to say that parental pressures increased once I came on the scene.

Dad, whose heart belonged first to the sea, eventually found the call too hard to resist, especially when faced with two lively sons and a live-in mother-in-law. The close confines of domesticity proved too much for him and while I was little more than a toddler, he reapplied for sea duty. Fortunately, he couldn't have chosen a better time as he landed a great offer to sail as a third officer on a cable-laying exercise in Fijian waters. Best of all, the company would provide accommodation there – a proper family home situated in beautiful surroundings. It was the perfect scenario for all of us. My memories are hazy but there seemed a real sense of happiness around at that time, especially for my mum. It was also a great adventure for Andrew and me.

We sailed out from Southampton by way of a luxury P&O cruise ship, the SS *Orcades*. During the six-week journey, we visited the Caribbean, passed along the Panama Canal, up to San Francisco and over to Hawaii before finally docking in Suva, Fiji. I feel sure the love of travel was well and truly sown on that journey.

On arrival, we were shown to our new home, an apartment with a fine view. Everything about it was more than we could have expected or hoped for. Better still, Dad's duties would allow him to go to work each day and come home most nights. For us it was just perfect. And so we settled in, looking forward to the next two years of Dad's contract, with lots of time ahead to enjoy this mini-paradise.

Unfortunately, the late sixties had a strong alcohol culture which, added to the long-standing drinking traditions on board ship, were set to spoil things. Slacker working days didn't help and Dad, at just 28 years of age, found himself caught up in an endless round of day-long drinking.

That level of consumption soon took its toll, not only on his job but at home too. Drink turned Dad violent, and fights broke out between him and Mum. They became so bad that, at one time, Dad tried to throw Mum out of a moving car. Things went from bad to worse. Dad sank deeper in depression, finally succumbing to a devastating nervous breakdown. He used to suffer with what I remember him calling 'Not There's' which I suppose were similar to blackouts.

Little did I realize that I too, would suffer from these same similar issues later in life. And for much the same reasons. Thankfully for me, it never got quite as bad, or went on for so long. In experiencing something so similar to my dad, I discovered a deeper compassion for him, one I carry to this day. It allowed me an understanding of his soul, so full, yet so torn over the years.

The result of Dad's problems was inevitable. That two-year contract and our Fijian dreams were doomed. It had only lasted for four months. The pressures, both at home and at sea, had built up and spilled over. Dad was fired and our little paradise was lost.

For a 2-year-old, experiencing this kind of trauma from my parent's issues would have effects for many years to come. I can remember a few things during our brief stay, that have stuck in my mind. I did get run over by a Land Rover one day, and can remember curling up and trying to keep between the wheels so I did not get squashed as the vehicle went over me. I managed to do this OK. I also had another accident where I fell off an old, fallen-down tree and cut my eye, of which I bear the scar to this day. I was also banned from going to a birthday party once as I was always trouble. I can remember putting some frogs I found into a neighbour's fridge.

I am still not sure why I seemed to be wandering around like this at the age of two, getting into trouble and having accidents, but can only imagine the trauma my mum was going through in dealing with my dad, and that she was not in a good state of mind. My brother Andrew was probably put in charge of looking after me during these days of playing, but he was only two years older so would not have been much of a carer. We did have two Fijian ladies that helped us out as well, Sinata and Raiapi, so maybe they should have been keeping an eye on me too.

We came back to England, settling in Portsmouth with grandparents while we found somewhere to live. Dad's company was honourable and offered him help via a London psychiatric clinic. Sadly, he emerged with no real answers; little had changed. In the end Dad concluded, probably correctly, that alcohol was his problem. And so it remained, with tempers and tensions within the marriage easily ignited over the smallest of issues.

After years of moving around we finally settled in Suffolk. Things quietened down and Dad was eventually able to return to sea duty. For us, it meant long partings once again, many lasting three or six months at a time. This was really tough on my mum, who was bringing up two lively boys virtually on her own. It didn't surprise me to learn that I was a handful. Dad would describe me as someone who was always 'coming back before he got there'. He always said that I would either end up as prime minister or in prison! That seemed about right. In reality, it was a classic case of a child picking up vibes from a troubled home life. There were frequent, violent clashes between my parents and the long absences took their toll on me too. I became so 'manic' that, at one stage, I was referred to a psychiatrist. Here my dad really put his foot down hard! He wouldn't allow it. His was the old school mentality, 'Keep calm and carry on – nothing is amiss.' However, in hindsight, I believe that, with treatment, I might have averted some of the dodgy paths I foolishly walked down as I grew to adulthood.

Gradually, I got used to Dad coming and going but I was also aware of the terrible toll it was taking on my mum. Home leave was awash with whisky and the domestic fights turned more and more ugly, with the police often involved. We boys couldn't wait to wave Dad back to sea. At least it gave Mum respite. By now, she was suffering from depression, her life dominated by nervous anxiety. And it was at these times, when the going got really tough and Mum was unable to cope, that Gan stepped in, ever ready and willing to take charge of home management for Andrew and me.

While life's pattern changed little over the years, there came opportunities for my parents to sail together on longer voyages. Again, Gan would step into the breach on the home front. What happened on those long, parental journeys we will never know but it seemed to temporarily patch up their relationship.

When I was 16 years old, Dad took me and Mum on one of those longer sea voyages. It was very exciting. We went around the Mediterranean, to Syria and Beirut, at a time when there was a lot of trouble in the region. We could see the shells going off in the hills, and on a later trip they had to leave port as the shells got closer and closer. I was somewhat disillusioned when we docked in

Latakia, Syria, and in front of us was a US ship unloading arms to the Syrians. Behind us was a Russian ship also unloading arms. This was quite an eye-opener for a 16-year-old boy.

I really loved my Dad despite – or maybe because – he was absent for such large chunks of my life. Even when at home, things didn't always go swimmingly, but those homecomings were very special as far as I was concerned. One particular memory I treasure is of Dad turning up to see me play five-a-side football, albeit quite a bit the worse for wear. I wanted so much to win that day for him, and I played out of my skin, and we won from a very big deficit, having inched ahead after a penalty shoot-out. Happily, my team won, and he was so proud. I wonder if he ever knew how special it was for me, having my dad on the sidelines.

Whenever Dad docked in England, we would all welcome him home with a visit to his ship. One such visit, in Ellesmere Port, was not only unforgettable but also marked a new low for us. By now, I was a teenager and enthusiastically joined in drinking the large amounts of alcohol on offer. All was going well until some local prostitutes came aboard, unannounced. It was at that moment Dad chose to lock himself in his cabin, for quite some time, while Mum, screaming at the top of her voice, banged ferociously on the door! Not the family's finest hour.

Even though there was an abundance of sadness and change in my childhood, I still hold on to the happier memories. Despite the trauma and the violence, I have managed to hold a deep affection and even sympathy for my parents. They had their moments of madness, fuelled with alcohol and often Valium, which led them to do some crazy things. But now I realize, life can be very hard for some people who often don't choose their circumstances. And it's all too easy to lose your way.

I enjoyed my schooldays and had a lot of good mates. If not the brightest pupil, I was certainly no slouch at school where I excelled at sports, especially football, and was very good at languages. Concentration then, as now, has always been a challenge. I'm easily distracted and full of energy with more than half an eye open for an adventure. Often the ringleader, I have survived many scrapes. I have always valued my friends, too; those who shared in the ups and downs of growing up. Friendships – perhaps not all of them wise ones – have played a big part in my life, as you will read. Where once I would pick pals up only to put them down later, I now value solid friendships. Without them, I wouldn't be here to record my story.

2

The Gamble

One of my oldest friendships is with Val, whom I met at middle school when we were around 11 years old. Real name Valentine, he was happy to have his impressive name shortened to Val. We shared a lot together in those teenage days, little realizing we would share even more in years to come.

We both left school early with few qualifications. There was no bright shining future awaiting us, we decided. It didn't take long for both of us to become disillusioned with anything the world could offer. Injustice; famine and deprivation; the unfair rich and poor divide – these were all things we thought about and even discussed. But they were also things far too big for us to do much about. So they were shelved. Cannabis gave us both somewhere to hide from thinking too much, the perfect retreat from anything remotely distressing. Dope was one more thing among the many that Val and I had in common.

After school, and for a while during our late teen years, Val and I drifted apart, each going our own separate way. I made the decision to join the army, mainly, I admit, to get out of taking A levels. One year of French and

German was more than enough for me. After submitting various job applications, it whittled down to a straight choice between the police service and the army. The army won.

My ultimate aim was to be a spy – a predictable life choice. Sadly, it was not achieved as I failed to gain the necessary linguistic points. Next came the offer of a trade in the Intelligence Corps, which I was quick to turn down. Finally, I settled on the Royal Corps of Transport, Maritime Regiment. It was the nearest thing I could find to being like my dad, and also I had gained a love for the sea. I worked on an ammunition ship and remember coming into Zeebrugge harbour one day, the ship fully armed and loaded. It came as a horrible shock when the captain announced over the Tannoy: 'Fire, fire, fire! This is no duff!' Serious stuff, I knew. Along with other crew, I have never moved so fast in my life. Had it not been quickly resolved, the ensuing blast would have taken a whole heap of Belgium with it.

I stayed on the ship for about a year and then in 1986, just three years after the Falklands War, I got posted there for five months. It was a wonderful tour with almost two months spent 800 miles further south in South Georgia. We worked on what was called a Mexiflote, which was a flat-bottomed vessel made up of about 126 various pontoons with two tractor engines on the back. This allowed us to take heavy machinery and supplies right up to the beachhead so they could be unloaded.

I was due to fly back in January 1987 but was desperate to get back home before the new year. We used to play three card brag a lot and I won £60 from the corporal who sorted out the flights. It was a good sum of money back then and I managed to persuade him to get me on the flight home for new year if I let him off the money. He duly agreed and I was a happy soldier that day.

While my military service started well, it didn't stay that way. Once I went AWOL for a week, earning myself seven days' incarceration in Marchwood guardhouse. This would be my first taste of a prison cell! The whole week was what they call in the army a 'complete beasting'. I had to run everywhere at double pace, getting shouted at and doing press-ups and all sorts of other exercises. I had to polish the floor and also my boots, which was called bulling, getting them to a high shine. I would spend hours on this only to have the sergeant come in and smash them all over the floor so I would have to make a fresh start. It was a long week!

The day I came to leave is one I will never forget, nor would the ones in charge who made me march around with my big suitcase held above my head. 'Left! Right! Left! Right!' the sergeant shouted at double time as I ran around the square in front of the guardhouse. As the minutes dragged on my suitcase got heavier and heavier. 'Get that suitcase above your head,' he hollered. As I tried to lift it up, I had nothing left and it came to rest on my head. The sheer weight of it then caused it to tear a little, and I could feel it getting heavier and heavier. The tear started to widen and still with the sergeant hollering at me, I could not lift it anymore. My arms gave way and the suitcase just ripped from side to side, slowly, as I was still running round. My head ended up completely in the suitcase and I could no longer see where I was going. The sergeant and the others watching were no longer shouting and all I could hear were peals of laughter! This was definitely a moment that we would all remember and recount over the years.

Towards the end of my term, I had started smoking dope. On release, I drifted down to London at weekends, meeting up with old school friends, some of whom were now in university. I both saw and envied their free lifestyles (or so they seemed) and slowly I became apathetic about the army. It was time to move on. It cost me £600 to buy myself out as I had signed on for nine years, but it was a price I thought was worth it.

Once reunited with Val, I discovered that, while I had served three years in the army, Val had done little more than odd jobs since leaving school. However, much more interestingly he had also travelled around the country in the wake of various folk festivals. And not always for the music.

We made an odd pair. There was me with my military cropped hair, fresh from the forces, and Val with his long hair and hippie hat. Onlookers would have been forgiven for thinking I was arresting this way-out fellow. Teaming up with three other guys, we rented a house on the edge of a Suffolk town. It soon became *the* place to go for all kinds of nefarious reasons. I was 21 years old with no cares to weigh me down. I also had a load of dope, so as far as I was concerned, life was one big party.

It was during this time that Mum and Dad were both due to go on another sea trip together, this time flying out to Panama and sailing from there. The day before they were to fly out, my dad decided to try and clear a bird's nest just outside their bedroom window underneath the guttering. The bad news is that he decided to do it after having quite a lot to drink. As he leaned out of the bedroom window, he lost his grip and went crashing down to the patio below and landed on his back. He was out cold and Mum thought he was dead. The ambulance was called and he spent the next six weeks in hospital with a broken back, and while he was in there he contracted a serious infection as well. He was a strong man and survived the ordeal. My brain was addled with dope and I was in my own world, and I always regretted not being there as much as I could have been for them at that time.

Working for other people just didn't appeal to Val or me. We needed a bigger, better incentive to get out of bed each day. So we made a decision to go into business together, settling on painting and decorating. It seemed simple enough, but we decided to take it seriously anyway. We sought out good advice, created a business plan and met with a bank manager, coming out with a £1,500 start-up loan.

Unfortunately, we received the money on the very day the Cambridge Folk Festival was launched and, before we knew it, we had unthinkingly spent more than £500. It was all so easy to do and a direct consequence of leading our kind of easy-going, uninhibited life.

Emerging from the highs of the festival, we were met with the uncomfortable truth that we had squandered a large chunk of the business money. Now there wasn't nearly enough to set us up. Reality hit hard; we had genuinely wanted to make a go of it. Now that big chance had gone too, and as far as I was concerned, there was only one thing to do: run. But that would take a bit of planning, to say nothing of funds.

Val and I discovered that our mutual friend Nick had received a serious chunk of money as compensation for a motorbike accident. We also knew gambling was certainly not an issue for him. We had often played backgammon together into the night. That, of course, was for fun. Never for £500. But this could be our way out – perhaps the only way out. I put the plan to Val, and we agreed on a strategy. We would challenge Nick and, if we won, we would have our money back. If we lost, we'd run. It seemed, at the time, a sane and sensible solution to minds well addled with dope.

And so Val and I gathered with Nick and some friends, meeting in the smoke-filled sitting-room of our house, prepared to take one of the biggest gambles of our lives. The air was electric, and the mood turned tense. Through the haze of pungent smoke and the clink of beer bottles, onlookers held their collective breath. All eyes were on Val and me playing against Nick.

Nick was poised to roll the decisive dice against us. His hands shook as he cupped the dice that could make him the richer while at the same time dashing our hopes of a respectable life. It had all started so well. Val and I had a 2–0 lead, and we could almost taste victory. But Nick had somehow turned the best of five games, back to an agonising 2–2. There could only be one winner and the stakes were high. Nick knew he had to roll a double six. His chances of doing so were less than 3 per cent.

The three of us had often gambled together but not with such life-changing chips. This time it wasn't just money. This time the dice would dictate the fate of the players. The winner would, of course, take all. But it's what became of the losers that would produce an almost unbelievable, life-changing story.

As Nick let go of the dice, it seemed like slow motion; the first dice stopped quite abruptly, and they gasped as they saw the six. The other dice rolled on for what seemed like an eternity. The next few minutes became a blur as Nick shot out of his seat with his hands raised, screaming, 'Yes, yes!' We all looked down and stared at the unbelievable double six on the table. It was all over.

Now what were we going to do? Where would we go and how to get there? The odds on a fresh start shortened dramatically. Neither Val nor I were in any way religious. There was a Bible in the house that no one ever paid any attention to but, as is usual, people do tend to turn to it when in desperate situations. It seemed appropriate to turn to that now as we really were left to divine intervention.

As Val casually flicked it open, he stared at the random wording: 'Go wherever I send you, without fear or question, for I am with you always.'[1] Val just couldn't believe his eyes, so he shut the book quickly, passing it to me. Astonishingly, I opened it up arriving on exactly the same page and passage: 'Go wherever I send you, without fear or question, for I am with you always.' We were both stunned into silence for a second time that day.

Right there and then, an unspoken decision was made between us. There was no time to waste, we had to run, and run quickly. Still dazed, we reviewed our options and soon the first problem arose. We only had £500 left between us and that wasn't going to get us very far.

Our first task was to go into town and buy a couple of rucksacks. All self-respecting travellers toted one. Emerging from the shop, we bumped into pal Steve, whom we had last seen at the Cambridge Folk Festival. Having explained all that had happened, it didn't take long for Steve to become equally enthused about our barely thought-out plan. He asked to come with us, and we agreed.

Looking back, we realize our decision was heavily influenced by the large bag of amphetamines Steve carried with him – the residue of our disastrous venture at the festival. In fact, we all got so excited about our futures, we totally forgot that it was Steve's hoard that had got us into this mess in the first place.

Having made our purchases, we went back to the house where we told Nick what we were planning. He too, was full of enthusiasm and instantly decided he wanted to come with us; the one snag being, he just couldn't face telling his girlfriend. So he just left her behind! The drug-induced excitement soon led to a mutual frenzy. Had we only stopped for just a few moments to think carefully about what we were doing, none of us would have gone a step further. We were, after all, four reasonably intelligent, down-to-earth guys, who had just done a little too much speed and smoked far too much cannabis. But all of that just didn't seem to count right then.

Nick also decided that he would not take the full £500 we owed him and very kindly only took £300 from us. This didn't deter us at all from going but only excited us more, now the decision had been made.

'Let's go straight to Heathrow,' said Val. 'We could get a last-minute flight somewhere.' It didn't dawn on any of us then, to go back into town and consult a travel agent. Sadly, that lack of reasoning is the nature of drug-taking. And Heathrow Airport was at least two hours away. Not to be beaten, we jumped into Nick's old car, rolled a large joint each and pumped up the music as we headed down the highway. There was no thought of yesterday or to-morrow. We were all completely in the moment.

Parking at the airport we found the ticket office.

'Where would you like to go?' asked the pretty, young agent.

'We're not sure,' answered Val.

This seemed to amuse her. Not the usual reply she had from clients. She could see we clearly had money but were not making a lot of sense. We could almost see her thinking, 'Who are these guys? Have they just robbed a bank?' Something didn't quite fit. 'Sorry,' she told us, 'we have nothing leaving in the next few hours but there may be some flights from Gatwick.'

Back we piled into Nick's car and drove the 45 miles or so to Gatwick. Once there we went through the same procedure at the ticket office.

'We have two flights leaving in the next four hours, to Lanzarote,' we were told by an equally bemused ticket clerk.

'Lanzarote! Where's that?' asked Nick.

'The Canary Islands,' she answered politely.

'That's paradise, isn't it?' ventured Steve. None of us really knew what we were doing but we all agreed it sounded a good place. Better still, the tickets were only £100 each. So we checked in for the flight.

Taking stock of our whereabouts, we realized we still had the bag of amphetamine plus some cannabis. Instantly, we agreed it would never get through airport security undetected. There was only one way of hiding our haul. We would take it all now, before we boarded. And so we all had a dab, and ate the rest of the dope. It was at this moment the unthinkable flashed up on the departure board: 'Flight to Lanzarote/Arrecife delayed!'

The next nine hours were spent wandering around the airport. Sleep wasn't an option after the amount of speed we'd taken. Restless, we wandered around, concentrating hard on keeping away from airport security. But with our wide-open eyes and erratic behaviour, we felt sure someone would spot us and become suspicious.

Finally, we boarded our flight, arriving in Lanzarote the next morning. The weather was fantastic and our rooms in a villa complex were really nice. The next three days were heaven for us. We ate well, drank lots, swam and sunbathed. We let go of the tensions of the previous days and relaxed into our good fortune. But it wasn't long before we spotted that the money was starting to dwindle. Alarmingly so!

Nick was soon disillusioned with it all. Just a few days in and he was having second thoughts about the girlfriend he'd left behind. Full of sympathy, we scraped enough together to get him on a flight home.

This seemed a good time to take stock of our own situation and circumstances; we had already decided there seemed too few opportunities for us on the island. Now, at last, we were getting sensibly worried about what we would do, as the money had virtually gone.

Val and Steve looked to me to devise a plan. 'Let's go back home,' I suggested. 'After all, the cheque books and cash-point cards for the business will have come through by now.' Then I had another thought. 'My friend Alan is in Ios, Greece, seasonal working. We could meet up with him and get a job out there.'

Alan was another friend from school who had spent the last couple of summers working on one of the Greek Islands. Why didn't I think of going there first, I asked myself. Deep down, I knew the reason – I had given up thinking at all. We all decided then that the best thing to do was to go back to the UK and then go to Greece.

By this time, we had met the friendly owner of the holiday complex in which we were staying. Val and I had both learned to play the guitar in the last few years and had brought our guitars with us. We had all played to-gether and we got on really well. We explained we had run out of money and, amazingly, he let us stay on until our flights were due. He even fed us and, in return, we paid our way by singing and playing music in his Irish bar. This went down a storm and eventually we were able to get a call through to Nick, asking him to meet our return flight.

3

The Journey

Val and I were very apprehensive about our return to the UK. We weren't supposed to be back this soon. 'Is there any mail waiting for us?' I quizzed Nick nervously on the phone. To my relief Nick reported: 'Oh yes, two business cheque books and two cashpoint cards.' Perfect.

Word of our sudden departure had got around all the wrong people, so on return we decided to keep a low profile. After all, we didn't intend to be around for too long. The plan was to get the ferry from Felixstowe to Zeebrugge, then hitch a ride to Munich. From there we intended to take a bus to Athens. If there was one of course! Plan B was to find the ferry that would take us directly to Ios.

Once home, we tried our business cashpoint cards but to no avail. Desperation was now creeping in as our situation seemed hopeless. Happily, back in the eighties, you could still present a cheque marked 'Pay Cash' and get it cleared straight away. So over the next few days we wrote out a number of suitably marked cheques for modest sums. Each time we were rewarded with funds. (It's surprising more banks didn't lose a lot of money that way!)

This certainly gave us some instant small change but not nearly enough for our plans. Neither of us liked the deceit of this, but the situation had got out of control and we decided we had no choice. Then I hit on the idea of presenting a cheque for a little over £500 and to cash it, avoiding as much suspicion as possible. To do that, I had to visit the bank; a smaller branch seemed sensible. At this point I was on my own. Val's nerves really couldn't take it, so he had stayed away pondering our downfall. Fortunately, yet another school friend, Charlie, drove me to the bank, the two-mile journey seemingly taking hours.

On arrival, I wiped the sweat from my forehead and took a long, deep breath. Amazingly, any doubts I had appeared to have gone. All I could think of was the necessity of getting money. I was focused and ready. Charlie parked the car on a double yellow line right outside the bank. 'Keep the engine running, just in case,' I instructed him.

People were in the queue in front of me. I glanced nervously at the car through the open door, hoping I wouldn't have to make a run for it. I concentrated on looking relaxed, remaining calm and trying to look confident, all of which was a bit of a strain.

A young lady I had seen on a previous visit rang the bell for my turn at the window. We exchanged pleasantries and, as calmly as I could, I handed over the cheque.

'I just need to check this out,' she said brightly and disappeared for what seemed like an age. I glanced over my shoulder. Charlie was still there, out front. But what was going on behind the scenes?

Thoughts of running crossed my mind but something inside told me to stay put. What was going on in there?

Suddenly, she was back. 'I've got the manager of the other branch on the line wanting to know how you will honour this cheque as, he says there are no funds in this account.'

I had already planned this outcome and knew what I would say. 'Oh sorry, we did our first job the other day and thought the customers' cheque would have cleared by now. And we need to buy materials for our next job, which starts tomorrow.'

Once again, she disappeared, seemingly happy with my response. She was gone for what felt like an hour but was probably five minutes. Then she was back, her face giving nothing away. Every possible scenario flashed through my mind as I awaited the verdict. She sat down and, picking up her rubber stamp, she asked me: 'How would you like the cash?'

Complete joy overwhelmed me. I had done it. We had enough to go on an adventure of a lifetime. Or so I thought in that victorious moment.

As I arrived back at the house, Val was slumped in an armchair waiting for bad news. I played him for a little while, then pulled the money out of my pocket and threw it in the air with happy shrieks. We'd pulled it off!

Strangely, even then, something inside me was not altogether happy with my success. Even in those moments, I was reminding myself that, deep down, we were basically decent people, honest and trustworthy at heart. At least we had been until just a short time ago. Val and I had been genuine in planning to get the business off the ground. But equally I realized, our brains were addled by dope and our situation had got wholly out of control.

The original dream was over, that boat had sailed, we'd all gone too far. It was too late for regrets.

The next day we got a lift to Felixstowe. Laden with our big guitar cases and rucksacks, we looked like a couple of budding rock stars. Our plans included making some money by playing music along the way. It was an easy way of making a quick bob or two. After a peaceful crossing, we arrived in Zeebrugge the following day. We had no real concept of how far away Munich was. But ever hopeful, we made our way to the nearest main road and held up a sign reading: 'München bitte'. It wasn't until we got our first ride that we realized why so many people had passed us by, laughing. Our friendly driver told us that Munich was at least 500 miles away!

The trip through Belgium and then down into Germany through the Black Forest was amazing. Pitching our tent together each evening, we felt free for the first time in years, not a care in the world. In all, it took us three sunny, relaxing days to get to Munich.

Even in those heady moments, we were vaguely aware of the fortunate, almost uncanny way we had been offered lifts and the speed at which they came. It seemed our plans were falling into place – or being put there by someone unknown. It was a comforting feeling.

Finally, we got on the train system, making our way to the main station in Munich. It was here we thought we would find out about buses to Athens – if indeed there were any. These were the days long before the internet. How did anyone ever get anywhere? Val was surprised to discover I had learned German at school and could speak it quite well. I confidently asked someone where the bus station was. Gratefully, we discovered it was close by.

We followed directions and as we turned the corner, we could hardly believe our eyes! There was not one but two buses with Athens written in the window, the first leaving in fifteen minutes. The first coach appeared very full, and the overcrowding didn't appeal to either of us. We could afford a little relaxation now, somewhere to stretch our legs, so we decided to take the second, leaving slightly later. We couldn't understand why everyone else didn't do the same. It was much more comfortable having most of that bus to ourselves.

As we travelled, we had time to reflect on the past two weeks. Having run out of dope some two days ago, the reality of all we had done was sinking in. It was as if something supernatural was happening – especially the way it seemed so easy this far. There was the money; the amazing lifts we'd been offered and even that Bible reading. Finally, there was the choice of two buses to Athens. Wow! It seemed as though we had stepped onto a conveyor belt of good fortune.

It took another two and a half days to reach Athens, travelling through the beautiful countryside of Austria, Yugoslavia (as it was then) and then into Greece. We played our guitars on the bus and slept when we could. Athens was a welcome sight once we had arrived after such a long and lucky journey.

We made our way to Piraeus Harbour and found a ferry leaving that night – yet another stroke of luck that kept us amazed and in awe of all that was happening to us. We arrived in Ios the next morning and soon found our friend Alan, who was very surprised to see us. It didn't take long for us to catch up over a few beers. Ios was a very pretty island; we could certainly see why Alan chose to come back year on year. It felt great to be lying on a beach again, in the warm sunshine, without a care in the world. Well, not at that precise moment anyway.

Our days there were spent in an alcoholic haze. Drinking into the early hours and sleeping until lunchtime, lazing on the beach all afternoon – then starting all over again come evening. But our money wasn't going to stretch another week – if we wanted this haven to last, we just had to start working.

By day, we started giving out flyers advertising the surrounding bars. Later, we would stand outside those bars and entice people in with 'special' offers. We didn't earn much, but it was enough to live on each day and to have some left over for a few drinks too. However, the routine of standing outside bars and drawing reluctant people in became pretty monotonous, so it wasn't surprising that we were more than keenly interested when we met some guys who had plans to work on an Israeli kibbutz. This is basically a collectively owned big farm, where volunteers could go and help. They painted an attractive picture of possibilities and to us it sounded like a great idea. There was one major problem, however: we had no money for travel and once again were on the edge of desperation.

To add to our woes, the season in Ios was coming to a close and we had no funds for a trip back to England. What were we going to do? Only one solution presented itself. Someone we knew from back home, who was also holidaying in Ios at the time, was going back to England within days, so he offered us his credit card. Later, he explained, he would report it as stolen. Naturally, our spending would be wiped off. In the meantime, the card would come in very useful. In fairness, both Val and I were reluctant to accept this offer; we had never done anything quite like this before, and it sounded so criminal. But needs must, and after a short deliberation we were persuaded. We felt we had no other choice than to take his offer. We were also able to obtain a second card, at a price, from one of the other travellers heading back home.

Seven of us left Ios that day: four Englishmen – myself, Val, Mark and Bill; two Irishmen – Pat and Sean; and an Australian called Tim. We had used one of the cards to buy tickets for the ferry to Crete where we hoped to connect with ferries to Israel. We arrived in the capital, Heraklion, to find we had missed the ferry by one hour and there were no others until the following week! The general consensus was to head for Agios Nikolaos, one of Crete's smarter towns and harbours. There, it was hoped, we could get a job and earn some much-needed cash.

A bit of searching revealed a most acceptable youth hostel but no jobs. So we sat around for a week, playing chess and strumming our guitars. As ever, the money pot dwindled alarmingly. There was nothing for it but to sell our guitars. Surprisingly, this proved easy enough and, happily, we got a good price.

On our last night in Crete, we decided to try out the card again and went for an Indian meal, even inviting others along too. The card worked well, and we were confident we could use it to buy our tickets to Israel.

Arriving at the ticket office next day, Val and I were both very nervous, so we put on a well-rehearsed show. 'You'd better pay me back the money when we get home,' said Val loudly and exactly to plan.

'Of course I will,' I answered. 'I'm getting £200 as soon as we get back.' We were hoping the ticket clerk could understand enough of our charade to persuade him we were genuine. In the event, and on request for seven tickets to Haifa, the bored collector clearly showed us he just wanted us gone, so he issued the paperwork with no problem. Within the hour, we were on the ferry and on our way to Israel.

The journey took about two days with a four-hour stop in Limassol, Cyprus. The weather was fantastic, and we lounged about on deck, eating, drinking and smoking – all luxuries we could only afford thanks to the credit card via the duty-free shop. While on board, we met a guy called Ray who, ironically, had lost his wallet and all his credit cards. Being broke and hungry is something we could well understand so, feeling sorry for him, we decided to take him for a slap-up meze lunch. After all, who knew better than us about being skint in a foreign country, wondering where the next meal was coming from? Once again, a trusty – if illegal – credit card worked its magic. If anyone had checked it thoroughly and found it was stolen, the owner would never be recompensed. So it was perhaps in everyone's interest that no one looked at it overly hard.

Over some passable local wine, we chatted away to Ray. He was an interesting guy who told us he was off to India to do some charity work. He made it sound very appealing and, in return for our hospitality, he promised to write and let us know about the local job situation. This was welcomed by the others too, who all agreed they would like to do the same sort of work – after, of course, they had saved for the fare. Had any of us known anything of Israel's tough military-style security, we would certainly have come up with a different plan.

On arrival at the Israeli port of Haifa, Val and I reached customs and handed in our passports. The heavily armed guard on duty started to ask a lot of awkward questions. How much money did we have and where we were travelling to? We tried to explain that we were sharing our money, hoping that Sean, one of our travelling companions, would have enough for all three of us and that we were going to work on a kibbutz and were sorry we had no supporting paperwork.

Suspicious as they were, after two long hours of questions, they inexplicably let us through. There was no earthly reason they should have done so. We caught a train to Tel Aviv and soon found a hostel in Ben Yehuda Street where we stayed for a couple of days. Happily, we were still successfully using a credit card for meals and shopping. Then, as happens, I became greedy and bought a quantity of alcohol for a party. And this time, the shopkeeper did a phone check! Nothing for it but to leave the goods there on the counter and beat a hasty retreat. We decided to then ditch this card and now only had one left.

Finding work became a priority and we found out that a moshav, which was similar to a kibbutz, paid a little more, so we applied. After a short interview at their offices in Tel Aviv we were offered a place at Paran, in the Negev desert. It all sounded rather promising but had we known then that our placing was in the middle of nowhere we would not have accepted the job. Strangely enough, that no-go decision would have saved us from the heap of troubles that lay ahead. But at that moment we were content. What could possibly go wrong on a melon farm sited in the middle of a desert?

With our directions at the ready, we boarded a coach heading into the desert, eventually being dropped off about four hours later. 'Where on earth is this place?' shrieked Val as we looked around only to see miles of sand and distant mountains. It was midday and the sun was at its highest, for the locals a modest 40 degrees, with a slight wind picking up.

There was a rough sandy track to our left and very little else. As it was all we could see, we started walking down the track. After twenty minutes or so, we saw the outline of some buildings. A tractor was being driven toward us by a young woman. Once in earshot she called out: 'If I were you, I would turn around right now' and, laughing, she drove off in the opposite direction.

Did she know something we didn't? We were all having doubts just as the farm buildings loomed up before us. It looked and felt like a long-abandoned town from a US wild west movie, especially with tumbleweed blowing all around us. We put down our packs and took stock of the situation. 'Are we sure about this, lads?' asked Pat, one of our party, in a broad Irish accent.

'What choice have we got?' answered Bill. 'If we want to get to India at some point, we need to save a bit more money and this is as good a place as any to start,' he added.

Bill was a bit older than the rest of us, and infinitely more sensible. He had co-ordinated the trip so far and had found the hostel in Tel Aviv for us. He had an air of authority about him, which was not surprising as he had just finished a short commission in the army. The others were willing to listen to him, and we all agreed to proceed to the moshav office.

Inside, we found a stern-looking woman who was obviously not over-pleased to see any of us. She greeted us by reeling off a load of rules and regulations, finally allocating us in pairs, to our allotted farmers. Mark and I were to go together, then Bill and Pat, Val and Sean. Tim was to join with another worker already there.

The farmers showed us to our quarters and, to our surprise, they were very pleasant. Our rooms had two beds, a kitchen, an eating area and a shower room. We were given tokens for the on-site shop so we could start off with some supplies. This was expected to be paid back once we started earning. All in all, it was very comfortable. Even better, there was an on-site bar, but it was open only on Mondays, Wednesdays and Fridays – the Israelis did not like their workers drinking too much or too often.

The working day began at 6 a.m., and rising at 5.30 a.m. came as a shock. But the sunrises were awesome.

Amid the barrenness, there was always the magic of sunrises and sunsets illuminating the camp – truly a glorious sight. Working conditions became too hot after 11 a.m., so we would pile back to our shacks for a siesta, resuming work at 2 p.m. until 6 p.m. In any spare time we had, we enjoyed free use of the farmer's motorbike and tractor. We had a lot of fun driving them around the fields.

Physically, the work was very hard – picking melons, banging in stakes for peppers, and attaching supporting wire in intense heat was exhausting. Other work took us further out into the desert, close to the Israeli-Jordanian border, where we worked in tomato greenhouses.

It was from here we had a closer view of the magnificent Edom mountains and watched the daily army patrols guarding the border. I found something mesmerising about that border and the regular patrolling, yet I couldn't quite put my finger on why.

The days rolled into weeks and the monotony of the work began to set in. We were all feeling an all-consuming fatigue. Even the bar proved very little fun, only offering occasional light relief. Most of us were too tired to even make the trip. It seemed all anyone wanted to talk about was melons! The guys were getting frustrated, and they needed a break. Tim, our friend from Australia, soon announced that he'd had enough and was going off to continue his travelling elsewhere, so we said our goodbyes and wished him well.

Most of the other workers on the farm were there for a working holiday and would soon return to their homes. Ironic really, as Val and I were there to earn enough money to keep us away from home. And that savings plan wasn't going too well either.

Some weeks in, it was Mark's birthday and we were organizing a party. This would offer a welcome day away from the melon fields and we were all excited. The local beer was called Maccabee and we started celebrations with a case of it – twenty-four cans between six of us. Not surprisingly, this didn't last very long, and we were soon off to buy more.

'This should do us,' said Val, feeling, as we all were, very merry by now. It didn't take long before we all burst into song – the party was in full swing. Being young, a few drinking games seemed in order and by now we were becoming seriously drunk.

'I'm p***** off working in this place for a pittance,' announced Mark.

'Me too,' said another. 'Let's get outta here!'

I remember nodding sagely in agreement. 'Let's go to India today,' I slurred, well under the influence.

'Yeah, let's go,' they all agreed. All that is, except Bill, the only one still reasonably sober, who pointed out that we didn't have the fare. Well, not enough anyway. The singing started again.

'Show me the way to go home,' we sang, 'I'm tired and I wanna go to bed. I had a little drink about an hour ago, and it's gone right to my head.' We changed the reprise however, to 'show me the way to go to India'. We were all in high spirits now and three cases of beer were soon gone. With little sense left, we simply staggered off to buy more. This was going to get messy, I thought. And it did.

In between the songs and banter, there was an under-current of discontent, and the same theme was repeated.

'Let's get out of this ****hole,' said one.

'Yeah!' they all chorused.

Lunchtime approached, but there was no mention of food and we had nothing to eat. Food had been the last thing on our minds. Perhaps, had we only prepared something to eat in advance, the next series of events would never have taken place.

Still in the drunken moment and out of the blue, I had a brainwave. 'Let's sell the tractor,' I suggested, looking at the farmer's machine standing idle, nearby.

This drew remarks such as 'What are you talking about?' and the more compact title, 'Prat!'

Before long, the songs had erupted again and were all 'row, row, rowing our boats merrily down the stream'. More birthday greetings flowed around Mark, together with drunken declarations of eternal love.

Again, I blurted out 'Let's sell the tractor!'

'What's he on about?' asked Pat, busy trying to cuddle the birthday boy to calls of: 'Get him off!' Gales of laughter filled the room as we tumbled around the floor.

'No, I'm serious,' I repeated, 'let's take the tractor to Jordan, sell it, and go on to India. We'll have some money, and we could leave here tomorrow.' In that moment, I remember being absolutely convinced my plan would work, never thinking the reasoning behind it could be all down to Maccabee beer.

'Yeah, OK then,' laughed Val. 'I'm in.'

Sean added, 'Me too,' before breaking back into song.

'Anything to get out of here,' agreed Pat as he picked himself off the floor.

By now the idea had really taken hold of us all, apart from sensible Bill. But then, anything might have been believable in the wake of the crates of beer we'd sunk. Bill's thoughtful voice did strike a chord but was soon immersed in more song.

As ever, cautious Val, emerging from his happy stupor, suddenly saw daylight too. 'Don't be so stupid – you're all drunk to the eyeballs,' was his verdict.

He was right of course, but I just couldn't let go of the idea. I was determined we were going to get out of this place. And we were, sooner than we thought.

My farmer, the previous day, had asked me to take the tractor to pick up his barbeque – borrowed a week before – from a neighbouring farm. So if anyone asked us any awkward questions, that's where we would say we were going. It all made such sense. Spirits were high – we were going to get out of here sooner rather than later. However, Bill was having no part in it.

'C'mon, it will be fine,' said Pat, who was getting really keen on the idea.

'Surely you're not serious?' Bill quizzed me.

'Too right I am,' I replied with conviction; after all, anything could be believed after that amount of booze.

'Well, in that case, you're on your own. You're all mad, you'll never make it' was Bill's final word as he sloped off, shaking his head.

'We're getting out of here,' chorused Pat and Sean, bursting out in song while not overly sure of what they were committing to. But there was no stopping us now! The decision was made.

As Bill retreated, the others staggered outside toward the tractor. 'Shushhhhh till we get away from the farm,' I cautioned. We all knew the farmer was taking his afternoon siesta and we certainly didn't want to alert him to our intentions.

The tractor was a John Deere 1650, a good old workhorse, with a 12-foot trailer on the back. I quickly jumped into the driver's seat while Val sat on the wheel arch, holding the top of the canopy. The other three – Mark, Pat and Sean – piled into the trailer, taking the rest of the beer with them. 'For luck,' they said.

It was after lunch and a scorching 45 degrees as I started her up. I put her into gear and moved off as quietly as I could. I had become a good tractor driver during the time I had been there – or so I thought – and felt very confident behind the wheel. Even more so, of course, with what I had put away. I reversed out of the farm and, with no sign of any movement by the farmer, I was soon out onto the dusty track.

'Woohoo!' yelped Val, feeling a free man for the first time since arriving.

'Are you all right, lads?' I called to the those on the trailer.

'Grand!' was the verdict as they raised their cans skywards before nonchalantly tossing the empties on the ground around them.

It was around 3 p.m. as we left the camp and headed along the dusty track. I drove through the fields, past the packing house and onto the main road, which was the only way through the desert. We kept to the road, rolling around drunk, tossing yet more cans any- and everywhere, stopping every now and then to relieve ourselves. Dusk was closing in fast, and the border was further away than I'd thought. Every day, from the greenhouses, we had watched the Israeli guards doing their patrolling. Unusually, this day, there were none, or so we thought!

Noam, the farmer I had worked for, would have woken from his afternoon nap around 4 p.m. It probably had not been his customary sound sleep because of the noise coming from our apartment. What must he have thought as he checked why everything was so quiet and his tractor was missing? We found out later that they had traced where we had gone by the trail of beer cans. I cannot imagine what he or they thought when they found out exactly what we had done.

4

Across the Lines

It had been much further to the border than we had anticipated. We were tired and sweating from the afternoon sun – none of us had thought to bring our tops with us! Of course, some of us barely needed to. Val was particularly tanned and could easily pass as a native Israeli. All he needed was to add the Star-of-David necklace he had so wanted to buy a few days before until I persuaded him to save his money. 'Save your money for India,' I had told him.

We had in fact, turned left at the T-junction, and believed there wasn't much further to go. As we rounded the final corner, our excitement grew. In front of us was a 7-foot-high barbed-wire fence; it was 5 feet thick. Beyond that, a 20-metre gap and then another barbed-wire fence of the same size as the first. To our left was a sign: 'Danger – Keep Out – Mines!' A skull and crossbones had been added for good measure.

Still in a stupor, I assured the lads that the authorities would display this notice to stop just 'any old body' from crossing. To the sober mind, that would have sounded ridiculous, of course. But in our collective dazed state, they all agreed with me.

By now, cautious Val was beginning to have second thoughts. In fact, looking back, he never believed we would take this journey so far. Deep down, Val thought we would reach the border and then turn around. Now he was getting seriously worried. Some encouragement was needed so I shouted out the command: 'Better just check the mines to be sure. Get some boulders and throw them in. If they explode, that should show us where the mines are – if any.'

'Come on, Si, don't be daft. Let's get back now,' Val pleaded. 'We've had a laugh and it's getting dark.'

But I was having none of it. 'Oh no! We've come this far so we might as well carry on. What do you think, lads?' I asked.

With the beer still flattening good sense, the reply came: 'Let's go for it,' and we started to pick up some boulders to throw, expecting an explosion. The bigger boulders were too heavy to throw, and the smaller ones were probably not heavy enough to set off a mine, even if we had scored a 'hit'.

'Told you there aren't any mines,' I crowed, absolutely convinced that the area was safe. This false confidence was somehow magnetic as the others instantly agreed with me – other than Val, that is. He was now getting extremely nervous.

'Let's go back,' he pleaded. 'It's getting silly now.'

As the others tried to cajole him, I stepped forward, put my arms round his shoulders, and said: 'Come on, Val. We'll be over in a minute and have all the money we need for India – we'll be OK.'

None of us had any concept of what it was like to live in a war-torn state. We had no idea of the region's history or the conflict between Israel and her enemies. Since the 1940s, the long border between Israel and Jordan had been used as an area of infiltration and direct military conflict. Consequently, many mine-fields had been laid on both sides of the Israeli-Jordanian border. If we'd had just an inkling of the true situation, even in our muddled state of mind, we would never have come even close to this place, let alone gone further.

Sean hurled one more boulder into the fences before us, and promptly deemed it mine-free. 'Right, get on, we're going for it,' I ordered. The other three jumped back on the trailer while Val just stood there, frozen to the spot. They're actually serious, he thought, and started to tremble. I looked back across the sands and realized it was a long walk back. The sun was low on the horizon and dusk was drawing in – fast! It would be night soon. At that moment, I remember the light breeze at my back sending shivers down my spine. We could return but the thought of wolves, which I had heard every night howling in the distance, was more frightening than going forward. Val told himself that of course it isn't mined, and jumped back on the tractor.

I started the engine again, reversing a little before putting my foot hard on the accelerator, going flat out for the fence. The fence took a dent but acted like a rubber band, propelling us back a couple of feet. I realized this was going to take more than one try. Reversing a bit further, I made my approach a second time, denting the fence even more. One more should do it, I told myself. On the third attempt, the tractor broke the thick of it and in we went careering onto the centre of the crossing before coming to an abrupt halt. 'We're through!' we all shouted, but as I tried to go forward the tractor stalled. Startled, everyone jumped off to have a look at the problem. Barbed wire was caught around the axle – and we were stuck in the middle of a mine-field!

'Try the toolbox on the side of the tractor,' shouted Sean to Mark, who opened the box and looked inside. To his amazement, there was just one item in there – a pair of wire-cutters! We spent the next thirty minutes cutting the barbed wire away from the axle. Once complete, I started up the tractor again, heading for the next fence. This time we got through in two attempts. Once again, we had to cut the wire away before we sped on our way.

Further on, there were some steep inclines and the tractor struggled in places. It was dark now and getting very cold. But we headed on, keeping in the tracks made by the border patrols in the hope of reaching a main road soon. At one point, one of the tractor wheels got buried in deep sand and we all got off again to dig it out. In the commotion, one of my flip-flops fell off and was buried but, after spending some time looking for it, I decided to carry on, barefoot.

To our relief, about an hour later, we reached a road. 'What do we do now?' asked Val, still in a daze as a lorry zoomed past us.

'We'll flag down a vehicle and ask where the nearest village is,' I replied. Just then, another lorry approached, and I stuck my thumb out. The lorry driver spotted me a little late but decided to stop anyway. His vehicle screeching to a halt, he stopped about 30 metres further down the road. I ran toward him.

Opening the driver's door, I asked: 'Where's the nearest village, mate?' The driver looked at me strangely, stunned to see a foreigner and not understanding a word I'd said. He simply shrugged his shoulders. No help here, I thought.

While we thought there were no patrols that day, as we had never caught sight of any, there must have been some sort of long-range monitoring to explain the next series of events, and how they found us so quickly. A Bedouin pick-up reached the scene within twenty minutes. Trying to take stock of the situation, those aboard it must have seen four bare-chested guys standing around a tractor and another man further down the road. At that point the Bedouin men appeared to have no weapons. In fact, as Val saw their pick-up hurtling toward us, he was hopeful that these guys might actually be able to help us.

But just at that moment, one of the Bedouin stood up and started firing his rifle into the air! Confusion set in as we tried to process what was going on. It had all happened so quickly. One shot, then two and more were fired into the air. The scene was utterly chaotic. The Arabic pick-up was right on us now, screeching to a halt in a huge cloud of dust that temporarily blinded Val. This was alarming – and these new guys were definitely not there to offer help!

Jumping down from the tractor further up the road, I heard the shots and commotion and quickly saw what was happening. It was either instinct – or stupidity – that took over. I knew I had to take care of my friends. 'Don't worry, lads,' I called out. 'They're only blanks.' And I started to run toward them.

Blanks, thought Val, why would they be firing blanks? The reassurance did give him a brief respite from the fear that had now engulfed him. Relief, however, was short-lived. Next, Val was abruptly brought back to reality as he saw one of the Bedouin brandishing and cracking a whip. Val put his arms up in surrender and then his whole head went numb as one of them kicked him in the face. Pain shot through him and, as he lay there, another Arab jumped on him, so close that Val could smell his foul breath. All thought had gone now as he lay motionless on the ground. Turning him over, the Bedouin produced some nylon cord from his pocket and bound Val's hands very tightly.

Through the haze and dust, I could just make out the shape of Val as he lay on the floor. Another gun shot rang out, making me flinch. I turned to see the Bedouin brandishing the whip in one hand and a rifle in the other. Close behind, there was yet another figure, this time waving a machete. Several more appeared, all carrying weapons.

At this point I realized it was hopeless. There was no ducking out of this one, we had to give up. Sean, Mark and Pat had already worked this out for themselves and were standing, shaking, their arms raised high in the air.

'Don't shoot, don't shoot,' pleaded Mark. 'English, English,' he added, thinking that might ease the situation. I too, was brought to my knees. By now numbness and hopelessness had taken over.

We were dragged over the sand and dirt wearing just our shorts. They bound us all with cord and blindfolded us too. We were thrown into the back of the truck and driven off at speed into the night. Every bump hurt as we bounced about with rifles aimed just inches from our heads – rifles, which we now knew, were definitely not loaded with blanks.

None of us dared to speak, we were all in shock. The Bedouin were all shouting at each other in Arabic, one screaming into his walkie-talkie. As I lay there, now to-tally sober, I tried to make some sense of our situation. What had we got ourselves into?

We arrived at their camp about twenty minutes later where, one by one, we were thrown to the ground. A Bedouin boot followed, kicking into my ribs. I doubled over in pain, assuming a foetal position for safety. None of us knew what was being said and perhaps that was just as well.

Looking up, I managed to see beneath my blindfold that Val was on his knees, his eyes tightly blindfolded and his hands tied behind his back. A Bedouin held a 9mm pistol to the back of his head shouting: 'Die! Die!' in English.

At that point Val was pleading: 'Please God, please help me! Oh, God, if you get me out of here, I will never question you again.' Time stretched like an eternity, as the guy continued holding his pistol close to Val's head.

It's hard to describe what happened next. As I was watching Val from beneath my blindfold, I experienced an extraordinary sense of peace and calm, quite unlike anything I had ever felt before. In that peace there was no thought, no fear, no problem, just utter restfulness. All of a sudden, it didn't seem to matter if they shot me, or Val, or any of us. Nothing mattered. I was wrapped in perfect stillness with no wants, no needs, no craving – just an all-encompassing calm. I accepted death that day. At the same time, I sensed that in his head, Val was saying good-bye to his mum and dad as he began to face, and accept, what seemed to be the inevitable.

Then from nowhere, I became aware of a couple of trucks come screeching to a halt beside us. To my left, a commotion broke out in Arabic. I peeked from my lim-ited view to see a man in uniform arguing with one of the Bedouin. Was this good, or bad, I pondered. I couldn't work it out.

The man in uniform barked out some orders and three others came from the truck. They picked up Sean, Mark and Pat and threw them into the back of their Land Rover. Val and I were next. Two soldiers sat in the back with us, guns at the ready.

'Are you OK?' I calmly asked.

'I can't feel my hands,' answered Val.

I understood as I couldn't feel mine either with the tight chord. Then, as one of the soldiers lit a cigarette, I caught sight of us all. Pat seemed to be in the best shape while Sean and Mark were stunned. In the brief light of the match, I also saw we had all turned blue with cold.

'Can you loosen the cords around my hands?' I asked Pat, who was sitting close to me. I was really scared about the state of my hands, there seemed to be no circulation at all. As Pat moved to loosen the cords, a guard caught sight of him. He turned his rifle round and jammed the butt straight into Pat's jaw. His head jerked backwards, hitting the side of the tailgate. He was out for the count. Right then I wished I hadn't asked.

Guilt was taking over big time as the reality of our situation sank in. All five of us were drifting in and out of consciousness, so none of us knew how long we had travelled when the vehicle came to a screeching halt. More orders were quickly barked out in Arabic, which meant none of us understood what was being said. Under orders, we moved cautiously out of the vehicle. As Val tried to ease himself out across the tailgate, his legs gave way and he crashed onto the floor for the third time that night. We called out to him but there was no answer. We were separated and all taken to different parts of the camp.

I was the last one to be led away. It must have been around 10 p.m. by now and it had got very cold. I started to shiver. I was taken to a room full of men and placed on a chair in the centre of them. One tightened my blindfold so I could no longer see out of it. There was a lot of laughter, first coming close to me, then retreating. Cigarette smoke was blown in my face. I couldn't understand anyone. 'English, English,' I was shouting.

Then, all of a sudden, a bright light was turned on which seemed like a spotlight shining straight at me. More shouts, taunts and laughter came from the surrounding men. A man with a heavy Arabic accent leaned close to me. 'What is your name? Where are you from? How old are you?'

I answered all his questions willingly, hoping for some respite, but it was obvious he didn't believe me. He shouted even louder: 'Where are you from? How did you know where the mines were?'

'What mines?' I asked. I wondered what he was talking about. 'English, English,' I pleaded, calling out for my friends. But there was no reply. Had they been killed I wondered? Events had now turned into a deadly nightmare. Was this really happening? 'We took the tractor out for a fun drive and ended up here,' I repeated time after time. 'I'm so sorry,' I added.

Again, I was asked: 'How did you know where the mines were?' The Arab shouted it repeatedly.

I later found out that all five of us had been subjected to the same harsh treatment and after some hours of interrogation, it became obvious to our Arab captors that we were all saying the same thing. The spotlight was turned off and I felt a sense of relief at the darkness. Any break at this point was welcomed. My body and arms ached as I was taken to another room. Val entered first, then Pat.

'Thank God you're alive,' cried Pat. Mark and Sean soon joined us. Emotions were high and we all cried with relief at seeing each other.

'What have I done?' I asked myself, shaking my head.

'Apparently, we crossed a mine-field,' sobbed Val, as we all shook our heads in total disbelief.

An hour passed before we were herded into the back of a lorry, setting out into the night yet again. Still blindfolded with hands tied tightly behind our backs, we felt every bump along the road and more groans filled the lorry. The four guards, each with a rifle pointed at us, reminded us this ordeal was far from over. Sometime later, the lights of a town lit up in the area around us. This gave Val some real hope as he had been convinced we were off to be shot in some remote part of the desert. A town had to be a slightly better prospect, he reasoned optimistically.

The lorry came to a stop, the guards motioning us with their rifles to get out.

'Where are we?' Pat dared to ask.

'Aqaba,' was the reply. We all knew where that was, as we had been to Eilat a couple of times. Aqaba was the southernmost city in Jordan, which bordered the Israeli town of Eilat. Prodding us like cattle, the guards led us down an old steel stairway. A large wooden door was opened and as the guards removed our blindfolds, we saw before us six dingy cells reminding me of old dungeons from medieval days. Val's earlier optimism promptly turned back to panic and fear once again. He hated dark places and was decidedly claustrophobic. Making matters worse, Val later told me he was especially worried about being raped. It was something he understood was commonplace in such settings from the books he had read, and the horror films he had seen. His muscles were tensed with fear and his thoughts caused him to shiver, reverberating throughout his body.

The guards then motioned us into cells by ourselves and to my immense relief they removed the cords around my wrists. I could feel the blood pumping back into my hands; it was like a bass drum and extremely painful, but it felt good too. I looked around my cell which was dark and no more than 6 by 3 feet, with a festering mattress on the floor. We all shouted out to each other in relief when we realized we were in adjacent cells.

Each of us tried to find a comfortable position in order to shut our eyes. But every which way I tried, my body just ached and the thoughts of the terror of what we had done couldn't be shaken off. It was also very cold, but eventually most of us managed to drift in and out of a troubled sleep. At around 6.30 a.m. the next day, a guard returned and opened our cells, beckoning us out. He had a smile on his face, which we took as a good sign. He offered us all a cigarette, which we gladly took, the nicotine rush feeling like ecstasy to us. The change in attitude was welcome but at the same time cautionary. Was this a good cop–bad cop routine? Another guard appeared at the old wooden door. 'Tea?' he enquired politely.

'Oh, yes, please,' we chorused. Hurrying away, he returned ten minutes later bearing a tray of mugs and, despite its red colouring, once tasted we agreed it was the best cup of tea – ever.

Two men in civilian clothes arrived, ordering the guards to replace our blindfolds. These men were much more serious, and the collective mood dropped as we were once again led out at gunpoint. 'What now?' wailed an anxious Val as we climbed into the waiting vehicle.

Twenty minutes into the journey, the guards told us we could remove our blindfolds. We were out of Aqaba and back in the desert. A plainclothes policemen explained to us we were on our way to the capital, Amman. Surely, if we were going to be shot it would have happened by now, I reasoned, as I accepted yet another cigarette from one of the guards. I remember noting how Val had touchingly put his head on Pat's shoulder and was drifting into sleep – his first time in twenty-four hours.

5

Locked Up

We reached the outskirts of Amman about four hours later and the vehicle was stopped while our blindfolds were replaced. Another twenty minutes or so, and we arrived at our destination. It appeared to be some kind of army camp – very modern and very clean. Once again, our blindfolds were removed, and we were each ushered into separate rooms. There, we were each given some food and water and, as I sat alone with my thoughts, there came a sharp knock on the door. 'Come in,' I ventured, thinking how strange it was that someone would knock! A young Jordanian came in with a pair of new shoes, a shirt and some trousers. I cleaned myself up with some soap I found in a basin and donned the new outfit. This was a good feeling and almost normal for the first time in a couple of days. Val and the others too were similarly treated and began to believe this was all a nightmare and it would soon be over.

One by one we were ushered into yet another room. We were all asked our fathers' and grandfathers' names. These were duly recorded on a card together with our own names. We then held our cards across our chests as photos were taken of each of us. Immediately I pessimistically realized that these were the sort of 'mug shots' often taken prior to going into prison or for ransom.

One by one we were taken before a colonel in the Jordanian General Intelligence Directorate. 'My king and your queen,' explained the colonel in perfect English, putting his hands together which seemed to suggest that they were friends. A good start, I thought to myself. He went on to proudly tell me he had been educated at Oxford. Some very obscure questions followed to which none of us could produce answers. Maybe, if we had been overly ready to answer, he would have smelled a rat.

After some time of interrogation, it became obvious that we really were who we said we were and had just acted extremely foolishly.

The colonel started to laugh. 'Do you realize what you have done?' he asked me.

'No,' I replied.

'You have caused an international embarrassment for the Israelis and made a mockery of their defences and border patrols. They will not be happy,' he said, a huge grin stretching across his face. 'You've crossed a minefield! You must have someone special looking after you.'

We were taken back to our rooms and shortly afterwards were visited by the International Red Cross. 'We have informed the British Embassy about your situation and the Jordanians are happy to hand you back to the Israelis. You will be leaving shortly,' they reported. This came as great news to all of us. Our blindfolds were replaced again as we were marched out into yet another vehicle.

Val could just about see underneath his and got very anxious as we seemed to be heading along another isolated road. He glanced toward the guard at the front and found his weapon was at the ready. Fear overtook him once again. Had we been lulled into a false sense of security, just to pacify us? Were we all being led to our deaths? Happily, his fears were put to rest as we rounded a corner and saw some sort of civilization.

Eventually, the lorry halted, and we were told to get out. Our blindfolds were taken off and, much to my relief, I could see the Allenby Bridge. Also known as the King Hussein Bridge, it spans the Jordan River and connects Jericho, in Israel, to the West Bank, in Jordan. Although at first I had been suspicious, I now knew that the man from the Red Cross had been genuine and spoken the truth to us.

'Form a straight line – and hold hands,' we were ordered. And having done just that, we were ordered to walk, very slowly, across this wooden bridge. Members of the Jordanian army stood behind us, their rifles pointing down the bridge, and we saw Israelis at the other end, doing the same. It was all done in slow motion, just like a movie, I thought at the time.

Fears of being shot were still flitting through our minds. Somehow, Israel felt more like home to us, and now we were nearly there. It was a great feeling. But it was also very short-lived. As we reached the other side of the bridge, we all smiled at the waiting Israelis. This was not reciprocated. Almost immediately, one soldier grabbed Pat by the arm, shoving him into the guardhouse, a rifle at his back. We all followed in like manner.

Why we thought the Israelis were going to be pleased to see us, I don't know. It was a massive lapse of reason on our part, and we were soon catapulted back into reality.

By now, it was about 6 p.m. in the evening, so we wouldn't get to know our fate until the next day. We tried asking the shift commander who would only confirm we would be moved on tomorrow. Now we all had time to reflect on the previous days. For some reason, we had all expected the Israelis to welcome us back with open arms. Our only greeting was a shove in the back with menacing firearms. And once we had thought about it, we were not surprised.

With time to think things through, I felt as though I had been given electric shock treatment – and I had just woken up! The backgammon game with Nick flashed through my mind – especially the way it had finished on a double six. That just wasn't normal. Opening the Bible on the same page as Val – that wasn't normal either. 'Go wherever I send you, without fear or question, for I am with you always.'[2] That was seriously not normal.

Looking back on the past few days, I reflected on many things; the way we had got the money so easily; the credit cards and the meals and tickets bought without difficulty. The seemingly synchronised lifts to Munich, and the two buses just waiting for us for Athens. Above all, there was the incredible way we had got into Jordan – crossing a mine-field, not being blown up and not being shot. And even down to the solitary wire-cutters found in the tractor's toolbox. I looked across at Val and, in that moment, there was the unspoken understanding that we were both thinking the same thing. It was all very extraordinary.

We slept reasonably well that night, despite our aches and pains. Next morning, we were given something to eat and on the Thursday morning a vehicle arrived at 8.30 a.m. to take us to Dimona police station, about 100 miles away. The drive was quite beautiful, and we daydreamed as we looked out of the window at the wonderful views – through Jericho and down along the shores of the Dead Sea to En Gedi. From there we swung inland to Arad and finally down to Dimona, which we reached at about two in the afternoon. On arrival, we were taken individually to the desk clerk where we had to write statements. Next, we were informed we would have to go to court on Monday and face charges of:

1. Taking a tractor without permission;
2. Having no license or insurance; and
3. Illegally crossing the border.

These were all very serious charges, we were told in no uncertain terms.

Put in a cell together, we settled down for the weekend ahead. With the exception of Sean, we were all extremely nervous. Court! Charges! It didn't bear thinking about.

'We could get locked up for years,' wailed Mark with a lump in his throat.

'Probably just deported,' I threw in, ever the optimist.

Inevitably, Val made it worse. 'Could be hard labour,' he predicted.

Then it was Pat's turn. 'You're taking this calmly, Sean,' he quizzed his friend.

'I'm used to it,' was Sean's unexpected reply, which immediately caught our attention. 'I've just come out of prison for armed robbery,' he groaned. 'I did eight years. This "holiday" was a coming-out present from my family.'

Not exactly a humorous story, it nevertheless produced hysterical laughter from us all, breaking the air of gloom.

'Poor sod,' was Pat's verdict.

During our stay we were fed mainly boiled eggs and salad which made me very sick on that first night – possibly an accumulation of days of stress. An Israeli was put in the cell next to ours and we started to make conversation with him. It was not very helpful as he painted a gloomy picture of life inside Beersheba Prison and Courthouse. He then produced some brown powder from his pocket, burning it and then smoking it. He offered some to us.

'No', warned Mark, 'it could be a trap.' It was the first sensible decision any of us had made in days. Drugs would be the last thing any of us needed on our records.

Saturday brought us a visitor. It was Noam's wife, who brought us our rucksacks from the farm. She was not a happy lady. I did feel quite sorry for her, although I justified it by thinking of how they had been completely taking advantage of us, working so hard on the moshav for a pitiful 9 shekels a day, which was about £3 back in 1988. That said, she had baked a cake for Mark on his birthday. Life without their tractor was going to be very hard for them. We all said a heartfelt 'sorry' and were genuinely remorseful. The return of our rucksacks brought a finality to our time there, as we realized it was unlikely that any of us would be returning to the moshav.

Sunday quickly followed and we were informed we were being moved to Beersheba, ready for our court hearing in the morning. The mood dropped even further as we covered the 20-mile journey and saw the large, grey building ahead of us. Our emotions had been all over the place during the weekend. One moment we thought we might be going back to Britain in a few days and at the other extreme – facing a lifetime of hard labour.

On entry to Beersheba holding prison, the booking clerk took our rucksacks and told us to remove any jewellery. I remember I wasn't keen on parting with my St Christopher, the patron saint of travellers, which had been given to me by my mum just before coming away. He or someone bigger had definitely helped us on our travels so far, I thought to myself. I never saw the necklace again.

We were herded through a series of high-security doors, all triple-bolted and made of reinforced steel. This did not bode well, as we all looked at each other, looking for some reassurance. Regrets were playing on my mind. Had I really been the mastermind behind this mess? If only we could go back in time, if only, if only. Finally, the yard door was opened, and we stepped through into a courtyard about 15 by 10 metres with 5 different cells, each with barbed-wire ceilings. It was a truly hideous-looking place.

Fear gripped me as I looked around my surroundings. There were other men drifting around, some looking as if they would be better placed in a mental institution. One man came up to me, frothing at the mouth and mumbling. I quickly realized this was no place to show fear. 'Get away!' I barked fiercely and to my relief, the man moved on. Others looked our group up and down, and soon identified us as foreigners. The fact there were five of us worked in our favour. A big plus for us. How did those on their own fare, I wondered?

'Cigarette?' asked one man, sideling up to Val in a creepy fashion.

'Don't take it!' I shouted, fearing there might be reprisals later.

As Val snatched his hand back, much to the man's annoyance, I noted there were no guards around. It seemed that prisoners had to be self-sufficient in here and had to look after themselves. This included any provision of food and we soon realized we wouldn't be catered for in here.

Each cell looked full, so we picked the least populated one. As we entered, the cell fell quiet as twenty-five men stared up at us. There were just ten bunks, all of them taken. Around the perimeter of the cell was a drain and at the far end were two buckets. Both of them full. The stench was the first thing to hit us. It reminded Pat of the sewers of Delhi. There was only limited room left – and it was adjacent to those buckets. It was going to be a long, uncomfortable night. I looked across at Val, who was still plagued by visions of being raped, and saw his muscles tighten again as he looked at the faces around him. I reassured him there were five of us and we would be OK.

After a tortuous hour or so, one of the Israelis came forward and asked, in good English, where we were from. This broke the ice, and the ensuing mood became a little less strained. We told them all our story while someone translated for the others. Crazy! We knew what they were thinking. But they shared their food with us and, for the first time that day, we started to relax.

Although we had barely slept, a guard came for us the following morning. 'Don't worry lads, we'll be having a drink in a bar tonight,' I called out as brightly as I could just to build their confidence. The trouble was, I needed some of that myself.

'Yeah, just like those bullets were blanks,' countered Val. We had by now had enough time to sort out our story for the judge. There was to be no mention of selling the tractor. That would have been sure to send us down, we all agreed.

As we left the prison confines, we were put into yet another truck and whisked off to the courthouse, about five minutes away. On arrival we just couldn't believe what was waiting for us and it threw us into a panic. A mass of photographers rushed up to the back of the truck, raising their cameras and clicking away in wild fashion. The flashes were blinding, and we all had to shield our eyes. The next few minutes were chaos as the police started shouting, eventually managing to bring the photographers into some kind of order, after which we were hurried quickly into the courthouse building.

'Wow! What was that all about?' asked Mark.

'We're famous, high-profile,' answered Pat. It was something we did not like the sound of.

The holding cell for the courthouse was dark and dingy with just one small window. It was roughly 20 feet square and it was holding about 40 men. Nerves were now decidedly getting the better of us all. Seeing the paparazzi scrum outside wasn't a good sign.

'Just stick to the story and we'll be OK,' we all agreed.

By now, my optimism was really getting on Val's nerves. 'If I hadn't listened to you, we wouldn't have been here in the first place,' he mumbled.

'Shouldn't we have a solicitor?' asked Sean.

'Bit late for that now,' said Mark.

We couldn't have afforded one anyway.

We waited for what seemed like an eternity. Then it was our turn. The courtroom was modern but formal, and everyone was looking very serious as we entered. We were put on the front row, looking up to where the judge would sit. Five minutes passed before the judge's door was opened. Someone shouted something in Israeli and an usher motioned for us to stand. There was a collective sigh of relief when a middle-aged woman stared down at us. She had a motherly look about her, which gave us the impression she might go easy on us. At least that's what we were hoping. She looked over her notes, read out the charges and asked us how we pleaded.

We explained we were always allowed to drive the tractor around the moshav and to our knowledge, no one was insured. We went on to explain that we were all deeply sorry, and that it had gotten out of hand. We also admitted we had drunk too much on the occasion of Mark's birthday. We had taken the tractor for a drive, we said. It had got dark, and we inadvertently got lost and crossed the border. Mark began to cry as the story was translated. We stood there, aware that we were all covered in dirt and looking particularly sorry for ourselves.

The judge listened intently as we all recounted the series of incredible events. She then stood up and went into a back room to deliberate. It seemed an age until she returned. We all stood up abruptly as she eventually came back in. This was it, we thought.

'I have decided to drop the charges relating to the tractor,' she said, 'and will proceed with charging you for illegally crossing the border. How do you plead?'

'Guilty,' we replied in unison.

'I hereby sentence you to two years, suspended.' And with that, she stood up to go, but at the last minute turned and smiled. 'Happy birthday, Mark' were her last words as she left the room.

We all turned to each other. Our ordeal was over. We simply couldn't believe it. Once more we were ushered out of the courtroom and back into the truck. The buzz was again electric as the photographers took more pictures. We had never been happier. But a little surprised and worried that we were to be taken back and returned to the cell. Shock then set in, overtaking us all. Had we heard right? Perhaps suspended meant something different over here? Happily, we soon found out that we were just being held while essential paperwork was being processed.

An hour later, we were taken back to the desk clerk, signed some papers and had our rucksacks returned. Then we were free to leave. It felt like paradise, and we all ran out into the street jumping for joy. We felt like the luckiest guys on earth. Someone had been looking after us and we liked to think we had learned our lessons well.

Of all of us, Val was the most traumatized and determined to get back home after what he felt was the worst ordeal of his life. Unfortunately for me, it would be a little longer before I was ready to go home.

After the initial excitement of our release, reality began to kick in yet again. We all sat around wondering what we would do now. Mark and I decided we had no chance of getting our wages from the moshav now as – let's face it – we had lost the farmer's tractor. However, the others were more optimistic about their chances.

'Let's go back and collect our wages, then go look for work in Tel Aviv,' suggested someone. Eventually, we all agreed. We arrived back later to a hero's welcome – if only from our fellow workers. The farmers, however, were very obviously less pleased to see any of us. And who could blame them.

After a night on the moshav and a lot of grovelling, Val, Pat and Sean managed to get the money due to them. This was enough to get us all to Tel Aviv plus a few nights in Momo's which was a very nice and cheap hostel, while we looked for work.

Life back in Tel Aviv was tougher than we had anticipated. Opportunities were few and far between and it took us some time to find any work. When we did, it wasn't enough to keep us. We soon sunk to new lows by way of begging on the streets which bought us a little extra, enough to cover our daily food anyway, and we also stole from the local supermarket.

It didn't take long for Val to become highly disillusioned with this chaotic lifestyle. All he wanted was to go home. So he made the decision to get himself to a kibbutz and work for his ticket home. By contrast, I wanted to try my luck in the big city.

So we split up. Val got himself work picking melons, during which time he received money from home, sufficient to buy two plane tickets to the UK. Delighted, he rushed back to Tel Aviv to find me and share his good news. Unfortunately, I had already left for Egypt two weeks earlier.

6

Egypt

During our time in Ios, Mark had met a girl, Chloe, and fallen in love with her. She had gone back home after her spell on the island, but they had kept in touch. Chloe had vowed she would come back to see Mark soon. And so it was a few weeks later that Mark waited with heightened anticipation at Ben Gurion Airport for her arrival, praying she would be on the incoming flight. Not only had he fallen for her in a big way, he was also praying she would bring some much-needed money with her. Fortunately, on her return to the UK, Chloe had got a good job in London. She had also saved money to come back out to see her boyfriend again. Helpfully, her father had given her a credit card for safe-keeping and emergencies. It proved to be very useful indeed.

Emerging from the plane, Chloe passed through customs straight into Mark's bear hug. The two of them came back to Momo's, where our chaotic lifestyle was still reigning. The endless stealing and begging, pot-smoking and partying eventually began to take its toll, especially on me. I was desperately seeking a way out, at last beginning to realize it was far harder than getting in. It was at that time it occurred to me I still had one of the two stolen credit cards to fall back on. The big snag was that it was still down at the moshav, in Paran. Desperate, I knew that somehow, I just had to get hold of it.

Eventually, Chloe and Mark announced they would be leaving us to go and travel in Egypt. I immediately saw this as a great opportunity for myself too. So, I managed to persuade them to take me along, on the premise that any expenses I incurred, I would pay back from my dodgy credit card currently stashed away in Israel.

Sean had left us at around the same time as Val, while Pat had decided he wanted to stay in Tel Aviv. So it was just Mark, Chloe and me who took the bus that winds down through the desert, arriving in Eilat some six hours later. From there, I hitch-hiked to the moshav to pick up the card, forever thankful that sensible Bill had it safely tucked away in his keeping. However, he didn't let go of it easily, certainly not without a lengthy, highly sensible moral lecture. But true to my hot-headed form, I just wouldn't listen and headed straight back down to Eilat and my friends.

The plan was to stay in Dahab, Egypt, for a few days, then head up to Cairo. Dahab was a welcome break for us all as we relaxed, swam, ate, and smoked weed. It was a complete paradise compared to the chaos we had left behind in Tel Aviv. One week later, we bought yet another ticket and headed to Cairo on the overnight bus.

Cairo was a big culture shock for me, especially after the time spent in Dahab and the cleanliness of Tel Aviv. The hot, dusty roads, the general bustle; the constant car horns and traffic going in every direction were almost too much to take in; as was the discomfort of walking around the many beggars lying on the streets.

Mark, Chloe and I soon found a cheap hotel, pretty basic but clean, and settled in. Later, we happened to meet up with a guy who was teaching English in one of the local schools. Danny had been living there a while and, importantly, he knew the ropes. This was to be very useful. He also knew an Egyptian, named Hamdy, who was one of those canny locals who could get us just about anything and everything we wanted.

This all sounded very promising to me, just as a new idea popped into my head. Next, I asked Danny if selling leather jackets for a profit would be a problem for us. He definitely thought not – especially with the help of Hamdy. The plan was to buy some jackets on the dodgy card, and then sell them on – at a profit! This would enable me to pay Chloe back for all she had laid out for me. It was a sort of Robin Hood gesture that seemed fine to me at the time. Danny promised to arrange a meeting for the next day.

Hamdy was a typical native rogue. Fast-talking and full of confidence, he assured us he could get us anything we could ever want. Naively, I liked his style and was impressed with what he was promising. We all agreed that I would buy the gear and Hamdy would shift it. Even better, he knew the best shops and right people to approach.

The next day, buzzing with excitement, we set off to the local shopping mall. We picked one of the busier shops. We figured that the more people about, the less chance there was of attracting attention. On entering, I picked out an inexpensive jacket and headed for the till. By now, I was quite confident at doing this sort of thing. I wasn't too worried, especially having identified there was an adequate escape route should I need it.

The young assistant didn't even glance at me as I said, 'Good morning.' Mumbling something under her breath, she took my card, picked up the card machine and swiped it through. I signed. Then, packing my jacket in a bag together with the receipt, she passed it and the card over to me.

Well! I just swaggered out of the shop, delighted with my performance, then made my way to the café where Danny and Hamdy were waiting. I repeated this performance for several days in a row and the money was flowing in. Everyone was on a high, especially Chloe, relieved she was getting her money back. Then came the day Hamdy unexpectedly informed me he could no longer get rid of the jackets. I was stunned.

'What are we going to do now?' I asked the others.

'My man has enough jackets for now,' said Hamdy, with a sly glint in his eye. 'But you can never have enough gold,' he added with a flourish.

Gold! It certainly sounded good. But surely it would be a whole lot trickier. Seeing my concern, Hamdy quickly added: 'Not a worry, it's no different from the jackets.' It was all right for Hamdy, I thought. It was me that had to go shopping and do the risky part, as well as bear the pressure. I pondered the situation overnight and then started thinking that this just might be a good, lucrative idea after all. It would certainly provide us with a welcome increase in income.

We met with Hamdy the following day, agreeing to his crafty plan. Hamdy assured us he knew just the right shops to approach with no problems. They were to be found in the Christian quarter of old Cairo. Wary as I was, it would be many years into the future before I saw the irony of his choice. The three of us set out on the underground train, alighting in old Cairo. Hamdy pointed out a couple of likely shops, making arrangements to meet up at a café just down the road. Danny and I were more than a little hesitant as we walked through the narrow streets of the old city. The intriguing, centuries-old history of the buildings we were passing was lost on us. We had a job to do. Finally, we identified a shop we judged offered an easy escape route. Or so we thought!

On entry we were greeted by a young Egyptian woman. She seemed friendly enough, so we browsed around various pieces, explaining I wanted a present for my mum. This broke the ice, and she began by showing us some of the nicer jewellery items, selecting what she thought might be suitable. I played the pre-planned game, saying that these pieces were a bit on the expensive side for me. I told her plaintively that we were looking for something costing a little less. Finally, we agreed on a piece costing the equivalent of today's £60.

I handed over the card and the woman produced the machine from under the counter. Glancing at the card, she swiped it through. Fantastic, I was thinking. Then, just as I thought we had done the deal, she picked up the phone, explaining it was just a routine check. I looked over at Danny – we both had the same panicked look on our faces. Danny turned his eyes to the door as I made a slight nod of recognition. It was definitely time to go. Then, quick as a flash, Danny had the presence of mind to rush back to the counter and grab the card as I shouted 'Sorry' over my shoulder. We flew out of the door together. Then we split – Danny went right as I took a left.

The alley wound first right and then left and after three minutes or so I turned a corner to be faced with a dead end. Right in front of me was the entrance of a very old church – one of the oldest churches in Cairo. But this was not the time to turn tourist.

Panic set in as I pondered my options. But there was really only one – to get away, I had to go back past the shop. Gathering my thoughts and composure, I slowly made my way back down the alley. As I reached the corner of the shop, I stopped and peered around. Everything looked quiet. There were just a couple of tourists window-shopping.

I braced myself and with my head down I bolted past the shop door. I didn't stop to look around, just kept going for around five minutes before reaching the main street. Once there I was able to mingle with the crowds. Winded and in some pain, I doubled over and tried to catch my breath. After a couple of minutes, I checked the coast was clear and, making sure no one was following me, I headed back to the underground train station. Finally, I met with the others at a café in Talaat Harb Street.

Discussing all that had happened, we decided that the reason we had come unstuck was going for the more expensive pieces. Next time, we agreed we would stick with the smaller, less expensive items. Hamdy then told us about another tourist area, in Giza, near the pyramids, suggesting this would be a good place to try our luck. Unbowed, we agreed to try it the next day.

The three of us met up around lunchtime. We were feeling fairly confident of the new plan as we took the underground to Giza. Hamdy pointed out the more likely gold shops, and flinging his hands wide, told us to take our pick.

Danny and I looked through a few windows, choosing a shop that seemed quite busy. The shopkeeper was extremely helpful; if anything, a little over-zealous. We sensed he wasn't going to let us go easily and certainly not without buying something. We played along with him for some time before picking one of the cheapest pieces. The shopkeeper tried to interest us in more expensive items, but we played the game by saying we couldn't afford it.

Eventually we decided on a nice bracelet which I once again said was for my mum. It was carefully wrapped for me, and I casually handed over the card. Time seemed to freeze in the next few minutes as we stood wondering how this would pan out.

Without even glancing at the card, the man got out his machine and the accompanying paper slip. He placed the card in the given slot, pulling the sales slip over it with a smooth motion. He then swiped over the card leaving a good imprint, passing it back to me for a signature.

This was looking good, we both thought. I carefully signed the sales slip, handing it back with a big 'thank you' while I stood there somewhat surprised at how well it had worked. At this point Danny seized the initiative, snapping me out of my daze by saying another 'Goodbye' and 'Many thanks'. We left the shop and headed down the road to the rendezvous and the waiting Hamdy. I held out the bag showing our prize and we all punched the air, shouting a triumphant 'Yes'!

Confidence was high once more, so we decided to keep going and try another shop. Hamdy pointed us in the right direction, and we picked a likely shop and headed in. The shopkeeper was the usual highly enthusiastic sort, just the kind of guy you would find in a bazaar. We browsed around, the shopkeeper close behind, pointing out more expensive items of gold. Together, we decided on a particular piece and presented the card to the shopkeeper who began to wrap our purchase. Then he did something we were not expecting.

'My machine is broken,' he told us. 'Just one minute and I'll be back.' Then quick as a flash, he was out of the front door and was gone. We looked at each other in concern.

'What are we going to do?' Danny whispered.

'Let's not panic, he'll be back in a moment,' I replied, trying to sound calm. 'I'm sure it will be OK.'

The wait seemed like eternity. 'Let's get out of here,' was Danny's verdict. But just as I was about to agree, cut our losses and run, pandemonium broke out. The shopkeeper returned with four other men in tow. And they did not look happy.

Bursting through the door, they locked it behind them. 'What's going on?' I ventured as calmly as I could.

The four men said nothing. Danny and I became angry, pretending to be the hurt, innocent parties. 'Give us our card back,' we demanded.

The men didn't budge. They did, however, inform us that the police were on their way. We looked at each other and, just as we thought of bolting for the door, two policemen arrived. Both our hearts sank.

It felt in that moment as if every bit of energy and hope had just drained out of me. We glanced at each other in despair. 'Your card has been reported as stolen,' we were told.

There was no real answer to this, so we tried saying our friend had given it to us, assuring them that it should be OK. But we both knew we were in a great deal of trouble. One policeman pulled out handcuffs and cuffed us both. We were then led down a narrow alley, passing the café where Hamdy was seated, waiting. We all looked at each other, knowing it was game over. We also knew with certainty we would never see Hamdy again.

7

Locked Up Again

The police van was just around the corner, and Danny and I were bundled into the back and driven off at speed. The station was only five minutes away and interestingly, very close to the pyramids, not that we were too interested at that point. I hung my head. I could hardly believe I was back in such a familiar position again. This time, however, I knew it would be a lot worse – the Egyptians do not take kindly to people stealing from them. And they have very specific ways of punishing those who do.

Thoughts of having my hand chopped off, together with going to prison for a very long time, flooded through my mind. The El Haram Prison holding cell was close at hand, and we were quickly herded inside. As the station door opened, fear gripped us both. We found ourselves staring at 40 other men, packed into a 20-foot square cell. After a bit of shuffling, we found a space in a corner and stood there, not knowing what to expect. We worked out that this was just a holding cell, so no one there had been convicted. This, we reasoned, could be in our favour, as most of the men would not want to make their position any worse. Even so, with a future so extremely bleak, it was a frightening place to be in.

I began to take stock of our situation. It was beginning to dawn on me, once more, that we were both in a desperately serious position. We had to have a plan. Danny and I decided we would stick to the story that a friend had given us the credit card, giving us permission to use it. We both realized this was a ridiculous explanation for anyone in their right mind. But we were desperate and needed to cling on to anything that might give us the smallest chance of getting out of the mess we were in.

There seemed to be a hierarchy within the cell and, as newcomers, we were pushed further to the sides of the area as we all bedded down. Around the cell was a drain which everyone used to urinate. Nevertheless, it was the only place left for us to squat down and seek some sleep for the long night ahead. Obviously, we didn't get much rest due to the cramped position, the stench all around us and the worry of what was going to happen next.

The following day, a representative of the British Embassy came to see us, and we told him our story. He said he would do whatever he could. Then with both of us handcuffed, a couple of guards led us out of the cell and, to our astonishment, herded us onto a public transport bus! We all received a lot of stares from the locals as the bus wound around the bustling, noisy streets of the town. We all got off in the centre of a very busy market, the guards steering us through the crowds to an ancient, turn-of-the-century courthouse.

Inside it was mayhem, with people everywhere. About a couple of hours on, the guards informed us we were in the wrong courthouse. How many courthouses did they have? There was nothing for it but to take our second bus ride on that day.

Finally, emerging into the dusty daylight, we were escorted into another building which this time, thankfully, was more obviously the right place. On arrival, we were approached by two lawyers who promised to get us off for a sum of US$1,000. Despite having no money, we readily agreed, hoping to sort something out later. Right now, we would have taken all and any offers that would help us out of this nightmare.

At around 4 p.m., the man from the British Embassy turned up. He was a welcome sight. He promptly got rid of the pseudo-lawyers and we went through to the courtroom. The case lasted ten minutes and, to this day, I have no idea what was said, or what mitigation was given. We only knew we had, by some miracle, been let off. How could that have happened? I asked myself. How could we have walked free? It had to be a miracle! It would be years into the future before I fully understood how it came to be. Yet again, at the least expected moment, I could see nothing but the work of some supreme and very generous being working in my life.

Free once again, I went back to the hotel and met up with the others. I looked terrible, suffering from impetigo with three big, painful sores running down my back. I was absolutely physically and mentally shattered, traumatized and exhausted. All I wanted to do was forget this nightmare and leave the country – *asap*! For some reason, Danny decided he wanted to stay in Egypt and take his chances. I, on the other hand, just wanted to get out and to go home. But I had no money whatsoever.

Meeting back at the hotel with Mark and Chloe was quite emotional. We all hugged and there were tears, mainly of relief. Having helped me to clean up, Chloe treated us all to some hot food and beers. She saw how desperate I was to get home and when approached, she readily agreed to loan me the fare for the journey. Such was my joy, I gave Chloe the biggest hug I was able to in my condition. In exchange, she gave me what I needed most – a way home.

As far as I was concerned, there was no time to waste. The man from the British Embassy returned and told us that he had signed a document of release for us both. But there was a rider; if either Danny or I got into further trouble, it stipulated firmly, we were on our own, and the embassy would have no more jurisdiction with which to help us. This scared me a lot as I still had some outstanding credit-card transactions surrounding the leather-jacket deals.

The next day, I went straight to the travel agents and managed to get a flight to Heathrow on an Egyptian airline for the following day. It was December 22 and I would be home for Christmas. I was ecstatic.

I woke early in the morning and said more emotional goodbyes before getting into the taxi for the airport. As I walked out across the hot tarmac, I realized I was still very nervous, half expecting to feel a hand on my shoulder. Or perhaps a policeman saying, 'Come with me.' I managed to find a seat and sank down into its comfort, still not quite believing my escape. Then, after what seemed like an eternity, the plane started its taxi down the runway, and finally took off. The relief was overwhelming. Home! Just the word sounded so free, so comfortable and so welcome. I felt sure in those last waking minutes, I would never want to leave home again.

After all I had been through, all the trouble I had caused and the risks I had taken, I was really on my way home. I had had my adventures and spent my time in the sun. Typically, I had challenged the boundaries and pushed them and myself to the limit. I could hardly take in all that had happened. Could I really lay all the blame on drugs, bad circumstances and even poorer choices? How had I emerged whole and still in one piece? Who or what had been guarding my footsteps as I ran away from everything good and wholesome?

At that moment I couldn't even think about it. I just sank into a deep, dreamless sleep for the first time in months.

8

Home Sweet Home

Four hours later, the plane circled Heathrow and I looked out onto England's green fields – such a contrast to the brown and dusty landscape I had come from. As I disembarked, I was aware of strange looks coming my way. Not surprising really as I was basically dressed in rags; a screwed-up T-shirt, cut-off shorts and sandals. Not quite the attire expected for a cold, December day in England.

With no cash at all, my only option for getting home was to smuggle myself on the Tube, going to the station nearest to my home, which was Redbridge. Then I would have to risk jumping the barrier to avoid explaining the lack of a ticket. Not a bad plan, I thought, and really quite tame compared to all that had gone before. From the station I should be able to hitch a ride and, in an hour or so, I could actually be home.

As the Central Line train approached my station, I started getting nervous once again. I was hoping no one would be posted at the gate. I climbed the stairs, moving quite close to other passengers, hoping I could squeeze past with them and avoid detection. To my great relief, the gate was unmanned, and I was able to exit without a problem.

As I walked outside, the cold December draft whipped around my bare legs. I made my way to the large round-about onto the M11 slip road. This wasn't new territory for me. I had hitched from this point many times, mostly in my army days, when going home on leave.

As I stood there, a thousand thoughts flashed through my mind. I marvelled once again at how I had got out of Egypt, and before that made my way across an Israeli mine-field. And most importantly, I had come out alive. It didn't take long before a lift was offered from a friendly driver who dropped me off close to my home.

And so I arrived back in the town where it all started, just a few days before Christmas. I knew Mum and Gan had no idea where in the world I was, or even if I was still alive. This was going to be a mighty big surprise for them.

Much humbled by now, I pushed through the un-locked door of home to hear my mum gasp as she covered her face with her hands. 'Si!' she screamed as she ran to hug me.

'There! I told you he'd be home for Christmas,' said my all-knowing granny, as Mum stared, horrified, as she took in my sorry state. There was no explanation then, emotions were far too high, just endless cups of tea and frequent tears – many of them mine.

Over the next few weeks, the family gradually caught up with my news – or at least the parts I deemed right for a mother's ears. Each related incidence would cause Mum yet more tearful upsets, followed by relieved wonder that I was still alive. Many questions, however, were shelved. I did not want to spoil her sheer thankfulness at having me home again. Revelations surrounding my survival would have to wait for another day.

There was more emotion waiting for me too, when I eventually caught up with Val. Quite by chance I had walked into my local pub and there he was, large as life. After plenty of man hugs, we were soon swapping stories and catching up on all that had happened to us during our time apart. It took some doing, as there was so much to say; no surprise then that the collection of pint glasses on our table gradually increased. We reminisced about our adventures. I was especially impressed by how Val had gone back to another farm and worked to save his fare home. I told him of my Egyptian exploits, and he found it hard to believe that, yet again, I had got out in one piece. I'm pretty sure that during our conversation he was silently thanking God he had not stayed with me.

Life jogged along quite smoothly and soon the summer arrived. I should have made those intervening months a time of regret and resolve. It was the right time – and I was in the right place. But instead of taking stock, all I wanted was to look ahead, not backwards. It could have been the perfect opportunity to make a fresh start with a clean sheet. I was trying – I'll admit not very hard – to settle down. I was back on my home patch, but sadly I was still looking for dubious opportunities to earn an easy living.

I was trying to keep away from the heavy drug scene, not always successfully. But to fill the hole created by my recent high-wire lifestyle, I became more dependent on alcohol to lift the gloom of long, idle hours. Still fragile from my travels, I tried to let life wash over me. But while friends from the past – both good and bad – were all around me, and boredom stretched ahead, keeping on the straight path became more and more difficult. Jobs were few and far between and I hardly had the sort of CV that would recommend me to a potential employer.

Those next few months were often spent round at Nick's house. We were still smoking weed, playing cards and staying up to 4 a.m., then sleeping until midday. Had we learned anything at all? Was it all starting over again? I asked myself. Gradually, I let go any good resolutions. I felt no incentive to look for a job as my mind was once again addled by dope. The only interest I had was discovering where the next smoke was coming from. We claimed our dole money and subsidized our smoking with some dealing – anything to ensure our next smoke was not just affordable but preferably free of charge.

As the summer of 1989 rolled round, I started to hear about some Acid House parties. I had never been to one, so I was really curious. I had been to parties of all sorts, but the Acid House scene was new to me. Following another festival in Cambridge, where I had acquired a taste for Ecstasy, I spent some months going to raves and fell in love with the dancing, and the euphoria of the Ecstasy. Lines had become blurred; the rights and wrongs were no longer clear. I had a need and that overshadowed every thought, deed or plan that flittered, briefly, through my head.

My thinking had become dangerously skewed. I never took seriously how involved I was with Class A drugs, which I knew, if caught, carried a hefty fine, and possibly a prison sentence. After all, I was only distributing to my friends in order to afford a free one or two for myself.

I could see no harm in that. It's amazing how we can rationalize our actions when we're topped up with drugs, popping pills or smoking weed. Life can seem so good, even blissful. But sadly, so short-lived.

The next progression, as I saw it, was to pull in some serious money, which led me to help with organizing and putting on a rave. Together with a few chosen friends, we set about finding a venue. On the Friday before the rave, I had managed to get a few people to chip in £1,000 for Ecstasy pills which I needed to buy from London. A biggish outlay, I recognized, but one I thought would produce some healthy profits on the night. A little later, we located a disused barn, just off the main A14 in Suffolk, a rural spot where we were less likely to be raided or interrupted.

Over the summer and in the midst of all the parties, Val had been seeing a girl called Karen, who had a 3-year-old daughter, Eve. While Val had chosen to keep it cool, I found myself very attracted to her. The chaotic life we were all living had taken its toll on her relationship with Val and they eventually called it a day. In the meantime, I knew that she had taken a shine to me. So after a big row between them both, they split up, and Karen and I got together.

Karen was part of the easy come, easy go lifestyle we were all living. So there were no shocks for her. Problems arose when Karen was evicted from her flat and needed somewhere to stay. You can't sofa-surf with a 3-year-old. The split with Val now made this a priority for her, if only for the sake of her little girl. Knowing both my parents were away on one of their long sea journeys, I immediately offered Karen their house. It would be some time before they were due back as their trips often lasted months. This would give me plenty of time to sort something out. Meantime I had a rave to get off the ground.

Domestic problems temporarily shelved, I was back to helping organize the big event and making plans for the London trip to collect the Ecstasy tablets. But first I had to keep my word to my friend Mac, to whom I had promised a delivery of cannabis. It was a short journey, as Mac lived just a few miles away. So, carefully placing the eight ounces he was due in the glove compartment of my car, I put the remaining Ecstasy money in my back pocket. Then I set off on the three short miles to Mac's house.

It was a glorious summer day, I remember. The sun was blazing down, so I wound down the windows, put on some loud rave music and simply rocked my way to Mac's. For some unknown reason that sticky day, I decided not to wear my seat belt. And, sure enough, as I came to a bridge over the motorway, I saw there was a policeman parked in his patrol car by the side of the road – just waiting for some idiot like me to drive by, beltless.

Once I had spotted him, I panicked, and grabbed my belt pulling it quickly into position, while hoping against hope he hadn't noticed me. I passed by the patrol car, slowly, trying to appear calm and collected. Once clear of his car, I glanced intently into the rear-view mirror, willing him not to come after me. It was just as I rounded the corner, thinking I had got away with it, that the patrol car slowly pulled out behind me. Within seconds, sirens and lights were beckoning me to pull over. As I made to comply, panic flooded my mind. 'Just stay calm,' I told myself as I pulled off the road, killing the engine.

'Good afternoon, sir. Do you know why I have pulled you over?' asked the policeman.

'No,' I replied firmly – a puzzled picture of innocence.

'You weren't wearing your seat belt,' he replied, rather smugly. My heart sank. He had clocked this omission and now he was going to make me pay. The police officer in question was one I knew vaguely by sight, by the name of Andy. He was old school, having been on the force for more than twenty years. I watched as he took in my messy ponytail, red Kickers shoes – all the rage at that time – and tell-tale, red-rimmed eyes. It didn't take him long to guess, correctly of course, that I was on some kind of substance.

At that stage, my addiction meant I needed to top up around every couple of hours, resulting in my constantly being stoned. 'Step out of the vehicle, please, sir,' I was asked.

As I did so, policeman Andy began a search of the car. It didn't take him long to locate the eight ounces of cannabis so carelessly stuffed in the glove compartment. I was immediately handcuffed, my rights were read to me and I was escorted back to the police station.

This can't be happening, I groaned to myself. How could I have been so stupid as to have been caught out again and to be back in trouble so soon? My mind, though still hazy from the cannabis, was now a maelstrom of thoughts and flashbacks, each one crashing into the other as my mind flew back over the last months. My thoughts went back to Israel, the mine-field, Aqaba, Amman, Dimona, Beersheba, Egypt! I felt it was all too much to bear and, not for the first time, tears of regret pricked my eyes.

Soon we were in the police station, where I was put before the custody sergeant. 'Empty your pockets, please,' he snapped.

I winced as I pulled the £1,000 from my back pocket. What were they going to do to me now? And what was I going to do? How could I explain it? Most of that money had been given to me by people for the purpose of getting drugs. I had to try and get the money back. Life was looking blacker by the minute.

Put into one of the holding cells, I had a sense of déjà vu as I slumped down on the hard, concrete bench that served as a bed. I put my head in my hands. I just couldn't believe what was happening. Once more I started to weep, thinking I must be the unluckiest person in the world – or perhaps the most stupid!

A couple of hours later, I was taken to the interview room where two plainclothes detectives were waiting for me. As I sat down, they slipped on the tape recorder.

'We have caught you with eight ounces of cannabis and £1,000,' said one.

'We also know you have been dealing in Ecstasy,' said the other. 'You're going to prison for a very long time.'

I swallowed hard and tried to explain the money was for my mum, for Christmas, and that my dad had given it to me. Dad was in Panama at the time and although my mum was due home any day, there was no way the police could contact either of them for verification. It felt like a safe option.

'I certainly haven't been dealing Ecstasy to anyone,' I said as convincingly as I could. 'I may have had a couple of free ones after giving my mates a couple of tablets. But that's all.' This was actually the truth as far as I saw it. I was no main dealer, I told myself. To my mind I couldn't see I had done something so terribly wrong. It was just a case of getting a couple of tablets for mates.

My reasoning held little water with the law, however. And because of my naivety, neither policeman could quite believe how easily – and carelessly – I had just fully confessed to a crime. Having never been in any real trouble with the law in the UK before, I was inexperienced in dealing with them. And after about half an hour of interrogation, they had enough to charge me with possession of a Class B drug and intent to supply, plus 'dealing a Class A drug, to persons unknown'. I spent the rest of that day and night in the cell before they released me, on bail, to await a court-case date. I had dropped myself into a heap of trouble yet again.

Emerging from the police station, I miserably contemplated my next move. I decided on going straight to Mac's to explain all that had happened. It was going to be especially hard when the bit about the confiscated £1,000 came up. As expected, it did not go down well. By the nature of drug-dealing, most of that money was owed by Mac to some serious others. For him it could end up very badly indeed.

In the event, Mac took a pragmatic view. 'Hopefully,' he declared magnanimously, 'we can make it all back with the rave.'

'No worries,' I assured him. It was then I had one of my notorious optimistic thoughts: 'And we may even get that £1,000 back too, as they won't be able to get hold of my dad to disprove my story. And even if they did, I'm sure he will verify he gave it to me for Christmas.'

Plans for the rave went ahead, Mac and I having organized most of this with a couple of other guys from Cambridge, some time ago. We had some DJs who would supply the sound system, and also had some security people who would watch the door and take the money. Spirits rose with excited anticipation, not only for the rave itself but also for finding a solution to our immediate money worries. The disused barn we had chosen for the event was well out of the way, the nearest house being at least half a mile away. Sound shouldn't be too much of a problem.

The cool summer evening of the rave followed a bright warm day. We set up around 9.30 p.m., just as it was getting dark. We had two good generators, one for the sound system and the other for lighting. Everything was in place, and we were hoping for at least two hundred people. At £10 an entry fee, we would make a nice bit of profit.

The meeting points for transport were fully arranged too, at three supermarket car parks around the area. Supermarket car parks made great set-up points as they could hold a good number of parked cars overnight.

I placed myself at the entrance of the disused barn, waiting to see how many cars would turn up. The sound system was great, and everyone was in place. Standing by were the

Cambridge crew, who were in charge of distributing the Ecstasy tablets. All we needed now were the punters.

At around 11.30 p.m., I looked towards the road and to my excitement saw car after car coming towards us. It was on! It was happening! I was buzzing without having taken anything. As the people arrived, we fired up the sound system and before we knew it the place was packed, and everyone was dancing. Better still, the money kept flowing in at the door. A few hours later, Mac took charge of the entrance fees, taking it back to his house under the watchful eye of someone from the Cambridge team.

Maybe it was the sheer relief of our plans working out, but that night I just let my hair down. I threw myself into the dancing and enjoyed the party, which went on throughout the night. But as morning arrived, so did the police. They had got wind of the event and had come to shut us down and confiscate the equipment.

Now down to earth, I was telling myself that it was still all good. The party had been great, money was made, and I headed back to Mac's place, still buzzing with excitement. However, as I arrived, I instantly sensed something was very wrong. The Cambridge team member and Mac were deep in conversation, and they looked pretty serious.

'What's up?' I asked. The thrill of the evening before was now looking more like a nightmare.

'We seem to be about a grand missing,' was the short, snappy answer. It appeared both men had gone back during the early hours to count and secure the money. The trouble was it only amounted to £1,500 – and we had counted considerably more than two hundred people attending. They decided to closely question those responsible at the entry point. Had there been a mistake somewhere? Either way, the much-diminished night's proceeds were divided up and each went his own way. No one was happy and no one quite trusted the other. It was definitely a case of unfinished business.

The next few days were packed with worry. I decided to go back and see Karen and her daughter, who were still ensconced at my family home. Mum and Dad were due back from Panama any day now. I had to find alternative accommodation for Karen and Eve, and quickly. Then, as so often in my life, things took a strange turn. Knowing we had to find somewhere to live urgently, we scoured the local newspaper and found a house for rental in a local village. Oddly, it was very close to the site of the recent rave, and I took that as a special sign.

Ever the optimist and despite lack of funds, I persuaded Karen to come with me to take a look at the property. Having found the address, we tentatively knocked at the front door and were greeted by a bizarrely dressed, grey-haired woman, who announced her name as Stella. She was very warm and friendly, and welcomed us in as if she had been expecting us all her life.

Over a cup of tea, we told Stella our story, explaining our quandary but also admitting we had no money. To our utter amazement, she offered us immediate tenancy, saying we could settle things once we had claimed our housing benefit! Such generosity, such trust. We were strangers, and yet she took us in. Did I see this as yet another small miracle in a life that had already seen so many? The truth is, I was too high to appreciate anything. Had I only stopped there and then to count the ways I'd been offered yet another slip-road rescue, maybe my story would have taken a different turn.

It would take a couple of weeks to get things in place, so I decided to move back home again for a while. There's no better place than home to hole up and take a long hard look at where you are and where you're likely to be going. It was easy on the pocket too.

One morning there was a knock at the door. Cautiously, Mum opened it to find two of the detectives who had questioned me previously standing on her doorstep.

'Is Simon in?' enquired one of the policemen. 'I need to talk to him. It's important.'

'He's upstairs still asleep,' Mum told him. She did, however, catch the urgency in his voice and showed him up to my bedroom. I often used to stay in bed until well after midday – not surprising when I rarely got home before three or four in the morning. There were many nights of heavy smoking and playing cards, so that morning it took some effort for me to drag myself upright and take in what was happening. Discovering the presence of two policemen at my bedside was far from a welcome sight.

'We got in touch with your dad in Panama,' one announced firmly. I caught my breath as the room went deadly silent, and I made a mammoth effort to brush any remaining sleepiness aside.

'Oh! Great news,' I countered optimistically.

'Not so good news,' came his reply. 'Your father told us that he did *not* give you £1,000.' There came a pause and then from the same detective came a grudging admission: 'To think that I had actually believed your original story,' he sighed. 'You sounded so convincing. What's more,' he continued, 'we have heard that there's money missing from the rave you organized and some of the heavy crew are on their way to get it back. One way or another,' he added ominously. 'So be careful.'

I wondered just how he had come by such information and why he would share it with me. After all, he had already charged me with dealing a Class A drug. Was he genuinely concerned for my welfare or was he out to get more information from me? I decided the latter.

So, there I was, my alibi blown out of the water along with the £1,000! To this information I needed to add the pursuit of the heavy gang, based in Cambridge, who were far from happy. Worse still, they were headed this way. All in all, this was a deeply worrying turn of events. I had no knowledge of the missing money, and my small share of the remainder barely covered my costs. Running through my head was the frightening prospect of them coming after me. And more to the immediate point, once the detectives left, I had to go and explain all this to my mum.

She was not overjoyed at my explanation of my current circumstances, but she totally agreed with my dad in the denial of the £1,000. And as much as I was gutted at the time, deep down, I had to respect my dad's stand for the truth.

Now, I had to go back to Mac and explain that, with my alibi shattered, we were never going to see the £1,000 again. That money was never coming back.

With no time like the present, I started out for Mac's place. Having brought him up to date on my latest misdoings, unexpectedly I found Mac sympathetic and ready to come up with a scheme that might improve things. It didn't take long for us both to concoct a new plan. We would get some cannabis 'laid' on us. This was the term used for getting cannabis without paying up front for it, so we could sell it, and use the money to pay off the debt due to the Cambridge crew. I was not very happy about this, as I was due to go back to court within a few months and, if caught again, it would not look good. But no matter how I tried, I could think of no other way around it.

Having fallen so neatly into the police trap on the first occasion, by admitting my crime, I kept myself very tight-lipped when it came time to attend the police station to receive my charge. What really stuck in my throat was, it was a charge I felt I should never have received. If I had only kept my mouth shut the first time.

One night, just before Karen and I were due to move into Stella's house, there was a loud knock at the door. At once I had a bad feeling about it, especially after the detective's warning. Mum, ever protective, gallantly played the game. 'Simon doesn't live here anymore,' she told them calmly to their enquiry.

'Well, do you know where he is, please?' she was asked, quite politely I thought.

She explained that I often stayed at friends' houses, sofa-surfing, and that she had no idea where I was right now. To my huge relief, the men seemed to accept this and left. At once I was ashamed of bringing this sort of trouble to my mum's door and told her so. I also promised her I was determined to sort this out and clear my name, assuring her that Karen and I would be moving soon, and this would never happen again.

Next, I went to see Steve. He was one of the Cambridge crew that was wondering where the money had gone and was seriously upset and angry. I assured him I had never taken any of the missing money from any source, and certainly not on the door. We took some time to talk things through and he gradually became convinced that I wasn't to blame. We parted on good terms.

Early the next day, Karen, her daughter Eve and I moved into Stella's house situated in a pretty Suffolk village. It was just after Christmas, and I remember thinking what a wonderful gift we'd landed – our own space and an understanding landlady. I began to feel the most contented I had been for quite a while.

The next few weeks were almost bliss for my little family as we enjoyed each other's company and our new surroundings. The housing benefit had been sorted out and I felt good about settling up with Stella, who continued to be nothing but helpful and happy with the arrangement. I also found out that Stella was a psychic and went to a spiritualist church. This really intrigued me as I had always had an interest in spiritual things. I went to her church a couple of times and Stella did a reading for me, which all sounded very real and believable. I was enjoying this new phase of my life. But it was never quite enough to keep me away from the haphazard lifestyle I had lived for so long. Drugs were always up there, as important to me as food or the air I breathed.

To my surprise and horror, one day after yet another rave, I experienced a sudden, totally unexpected, nerve-shredding panic attack, so severe I thought I was about to die. I didn't know at that point it was merely a panic attack – it felt so much worse, and I was very frightened. I retreated back to Stella's house where I felt safe. I welcomed her reassurances and eventually got through it. Some days later, and thanks to Stella, I was referred to a clairvoyant who taught me the principles of chakra meditation, which helped me feel really good about myself and my life – for a short time, anyway.

I continued to practise chakra meditation for a couple of months or more, although aware it was doing little for my thinking or reasoning. The chakras are what Hindus believe to be seven energy centres within the body, and that to meditate on them in this way energizes them and gives you a feeling of well-being. To pay for the sessions I had continued to deal in cannabis. It was very little help financially, but as a prop it was crucial.

In all of this, I was aware that the date of my court case was barely two months away. It caused a great amount of tension. Sadly, it was at this point Stella decided to sell her house and Karen and I had to move on. Fortunately, it didn't take long to find another little house to rent in a nearby, equally pretty village. The new home was called Connemara, which Karen and I thought was not only a pretty name but boded well for our future, as we experienced a new-found peace there.

My days at Connemara were happy ones, although they did not last very long. I was suffering with increasing stress as the date of my court case crept ever closer. The tension in the house grew to such a boiling point that the relationship broke down and, sadly, we decided to part company. For me, that meant the extra pressure of yet again returning to the family home.

9

Norwich

By now my dad had come home from sea and it was actually pleasant to be around him and Mum as we spent family time together. As the days passed, I realized that, in my own mind, I had never contemplated going to prison for my crime. I reasoned this was my first offence (well, in the UK anyway!). My solicitor, however, thought differently. He squashed my optimism with the caution that there was a very good chance prison would be the outcome.

On the day of the case, my mum woke up weeping. She had a really bad feeling as to how things would turn out. Ever the loving Mum, she cooked a good, full English breakfast for me as she held back her tears. My dad was also on hand to take me to crown court to face what could no longer be avoided.

We set off early to ensure we would be there on time, my thoughts still erring on the side of leniency, despite the seriousness of the case. We didn't have to wait long before we were called into the courtroom where the charges were read out.

'You have been charged with possession of a Class B drug with intent to supply; and intent to supply a Class A drug to persons unknown. How do you plead?' barked the imposing judge.

'Guilty,' I replied.

The year 1990 was not the best time to be up in court on drug offences. The crackdown on substances and the whole rave scene had come under the radar of Margaret Thatcher's government and the general mood veered to making examples of offenders.

Which way would things go, I pondered? As I had pleaded guilty, we now came to the mitigation part of the process. I felt sure this would go in my favour. For the past two months or so, I had been working part-time at a local old people's home and got on well with the owners, David and Betty. Both were Christians and I had confided in David about the upcoming court case. He had proved very understanding and compassionate, and was also in court today for support. David had prepared a good character reference for me, which he read out. The judge listened carefully and then a deafening hush fell on the court.

'Dealing in drugs is a serious matter,' said the judge, in a tone that didn't sound overly comforting.

Still optimistic, I waited patiently for what was to come next. After all, I pondered, I had only got the stuff for friends. This was beginning to make me sound like a major drug dealer. My heart wavered for a second time as the judge continued: 'I have listened to your character reference and your plea and have taken into consideration your intention of changing your life for the better. However,' – that word again. It seemed to hang in the air for an eternity and something in my heart turned cold. Time froze.

'However, I cannot overlook the seriousness of these charges and I will have to impose a custodial sentence on you.' The court was hushed, and I just stared at the judge in disbelief as he continued: 'I sentence you to thirty months' imprisonment. Take him down.'

Once again, my eyes filled with tears as I glanced at my dad on my way to the cells. Thirty months! That's two and a half years! Once down in the holding cell, I was crying hysterically. I wasn't a big criminal, I told myself. This was my first-ever offence. This was so unfair.

My dad was allowed to come and see me. He was devastated to see his youngest son facing a prison term. Even though he did not agree with what I had done, seeing a child being sent to prison is something no parent should have to go through. How would he break the news to Mum, who was waiting at home?

Dad was allowed to stay with me for about half an hour. Not much was said during that time. We just stared at each other in deep disbelief. Thankfully, my solicitor entered the scene to explain that I would only have to serve ten months of the sentence if I gained my parole. I should have been cheered by this news. But it was still prison. A great chunk of my life had been taken from me.

Despite all that had gone before, all the multiple times I had escaped justice by a whisker, finally it had caught up with me. I reviewed the risks I had taken, the stealing, the drugs, the scrapes and the chances. Was this to be the reckoning?

How could I have known then that the next few months in prison would actually offer me a far more positive future? In my misery, all I saw were the unknown horrors waiting for me behind those strong iron doors. Ironically, I wondered how I would survive without the drugs that had got me here in the first place.

As I was led away, handcuffed to another prisoner, the whole episode felt surreal to me. I was still in a state of shock as we boarded the transport that would take us to Norwich Prison, soon to be my new digs. Looking out of the window sent a shiver down my spine as I gazed at the formidable building ahead. Built in 1887, it formed part of the penal system brought about by the great prison reformer, Elizabeth Fry. Not that I was impressed at the time.

The transfer to prison was made by coach as no prison vans were available that day. It reminded me of another trip to prison – one taken in a different country, at a different time, and by very different transport: a public bus service, no less.

On arrival, we were ushered into a holding room and told to strip off. The cuffs were removed as the door slammed shut behind us. My head in a daze, I put on my prison uniform and collected my bedding. From there I was escorted to a holding cell for the night.

As the guards locked the door, I realized I was still in disbelief, even denial. My thoughts crowded in as I recalled the adventures of the past months. The mine-fields, the jails, the Israelis and Egyptians, the drugs, the raves and the parties. Now I was locked in an old and rather frightening Victorian prison, in deepest Norfolk, totally alone.

It was all too much; I hung my head and simply sobbed. I remember wondering, was this a test, or a lesson they were trying to teach me? Maybe they would let me out in the morning? Such thoughts, however, were soon dispelled as the following morning I was put in a permanent cell on the fourth landing. I discovered that this prison was just a holding facility while they decided which prison they would eventually send me to, and possibly not my final destination. Note: In the 1990s prisoners only had to serve a third of their time. Later, it would be put up to a half.

There were no toilets in the cells at this point, so slopping-out became the norm each morning. Despite the shock, this actually turned out to be a good time to see other prisoners as we made our way to the washrooms, complete with buckets, bearing the previous night's waste.

I did my best to settle in and keep myself to myself. I always had the knack of getting on with people, rarely upsetting anyone or letting anyone upset me. Soon, I befriended a guy called Bob from my home-town. He shared the local paper with me, which made it feel as if I hadn't entirely lost touch with all reality. We got on really well.

'You don't want to go to Wayland Prison,' advised my new friend. 'The Annexe is the best place, if you can get it.'

The Annexe was another part of the prison complex. A lower Category C section, it had dormitories and windows but no cells. The doors weren't locked during the day, and inmates could move about the complex, which included a nice garden and field surrounded by a perimeter fence. This all sounded good to me, so I really pinned my hopes on being sent there. It also gave me even more of an incentive to keep my head down and my nose clean. That would contrast with others I had seen. The loud and abusive, I was advised, were generally sent to Wayland.

Despite the shock of the experience, prison reality soon settled in, and the first weeks went by quite quickly. I buckled down and got used to the routine while I waited to see where I would eventually be sent. I got on well with my fellow prisoners, especially Bob who had been here before and knew all the ropes.

Bob's sentence on this occasion was only a short one, but I really appreciated all his advice and the way he took me under his wing. It was something I would look back on and, in time, thank God for his provision.

The day of my possible transfer dawned. Where would they send me? A prison officer came into my cell to announce my destination. I gained nothing by looking at his face. There was a pause – then: 'Right, Williams, pack up your things, we are moving you to the Annexe.'

'Thanks, guv,' I breathed. Fantastic! This was the best news, and I wasted no time in gathering my things together in case they changed their minds.

The Annexe was at the south-west of the older prison, which was called Britannia Annexe. It was part of the Royal Norfolk Regiment depot, which had been converted into a prison in the 1970s, specifically to hold Category C prisoners. The dormitories, which held around twenty-two men on double bunks, at least offered some privacy, as the prisoners could partition off their own small areas. It's amazing how you can come to terms with your circumstances and be grateful for even the smallest of blessings.

I settled in quickly and really appreciated the sense of freedom brought by not being locked in a cell. We could go out in the daytime and stroll around the grounds when we weren't working. There was a pool room, TV room, showers and toilets, even a bathhouse when you needed a good soak. The biggest bonus was, of course, not having to slop out each day.

I got a job in the bookbinding section where I was trained on an old Heidelberg printing-press. I found I almost enjoyed it, as we printed leaflets for local companies. This 'job' paid about £3.50 a week, not a huge sum but handy for my tobacco. I made a conscious decision not to smoke cannabis in prison. Not only was it very expensive but also I soon saw how easy it was for those who depended on it to get themselves into deep difficulties. This was especially true when prisoners were forced to borrow to feed their habit.

Owing money in prison is never a good idea, so learning to manage the little you had was sound prison wisdom. The biggest incentive to avoiding the weed was seeing how quickly and brutally men got into trouble. One smoke could cost around £5 and there were a lot of beatings come Wednesdays – canteen day – when a prisoner couldn't make his payback.

I started each day with a 3-mile run around the perimeter fence. This was followed by breakfast, which usually consisted of porridge with jam and a couple of rounds of toast. The banter was relentless, but you had to stay sharp, otherwise others would swiftly take advantage of you.

Being locked away gave me plenty of time to think, especially over the past two years and all that I had been through. I thought too about the lives I had touched, the people I had hurt and the many foolish crimes I had committed. There came a deep realization that being here in prison was as low as I ever wanted to reach. I knew I had to do something radical about changing my chaotic life.

I had always had an interest in spiritual things, and this became more important to me with time to spare. I meditated and read lots of different books. I started to go to chapel each Sunday, which I found interesting. In addition, I used to practise the chakra meditation, twice a day and mostly at night. For this, I found a quiet spot, just outside the chapel doors, up a windy metal staircase – somewhere nobody went after dark.

This interest in spiritual things had started before I came into prison. I had sat one night, meditating in my bedroom, when I felt a surge rush through my body. It certainly wasn't a bad sensation; in fact, it was quite pleasant. Curious, I had phoned my meditation teacher who explained it was an energy surge. This also happened when I was meditating in the prison one day.

In my spare time, I had been pondering on the reality of God and a higher being. Gradually, it became more and more real to me as now I had the time to look back and take some meaning from all that had happened to me. I became aware that it was nothing short of a miracle that I was alive at all! Who crosses mine-fields and survives, I asked myself? Who gets caught and escapes a Jordanian prison? Who steals from Egyptians and gets away with it? I should have died several times or, at the very least, I could still be locked in a foreign prison – with the key thrown away.

Surely, there just had to be a God, I told myself.

I filled my time with work, reading books, writing letters and playing football. I was also running and going regularly to chapel. The thought of parole was constantly in my thoughts – would I have to wait until I had served ten months, or twenty months? The latter was a horrible thought – one that consumed my mind.

As it was, chapel began to play a bigger and bigger role in my life. As I listened to the teaching, I decided I would be baptized as a public show of my new-found belief in God. There was little in the way of planning, and a random date was chosen. By sheer coincidence, it was 9 December 1990, which was roughly one year on from the rave that we had organized. Another sign of something supernatural going on, I mused.

Years later, when I look back at that baptism, I realize that although I sincerely believed in God at the time, I didn't really see the need to repent or be too ashamed of anything in my life. I saw myself then as a jolly good guy; one who people liked and who got on well with them, even if others might see a different Simon. I was, after all, a kind person, good-hearted and always ready to help someone in need. So when it came to the part in the ceremony where the vicar asked me what I was sorry for, the worst I could think of then was maybe stealing a pen from a friend when I was younger.

The fact that I was in prison for dealing drugs just didn't seem too bad – it wasn't an awful crime. Let's face it, I was among friends, and we had all done a bit of something wrong in our youth. At that time, I thought I was just unlucky to have been caught. This twisted view would, of course, radically change over the years. But right then, the baptism went ahead, and I confidently proclaimed my faith in Jesus Christ.

Three months into my sentence, I got friendly with Mark, a guy from London. We got on really well, laughing a lot together. We had a good deal in common too, especially the rave scene. But there was a snag. Mark still liked to smoke a spliff and I hadn't done so for more than three months, my abstinence driven by what I saw around me.

But temptation was everywhere. 'Go on, have a puff,' Mark would constantly goad me. My initial fear of prison was subsiding. I was settling in, going to the gym and playing football as well as attending chapel. I was meditating too. But it was still prison and I had to keep my nose clean as I had my parole to think about.

Inevitably, within weeks, the usual boredom of prison life set in. Everything was overshadowed by the question of whether I would get parole, or not. On the one hand, I could be out in five months – on the other, another year or so. This thinking just crippled my mind. I constantly bombarded everyone I saw, including the officers, asking what they thought of my chances. Most were kind and tried to reassure me, saying it would all be OK.

But there were others who would warn: 'The parole board doesn't like drug charges, so your chances look slim!' The pressure was building, and I could feel myself getting more and more wound up. It was just such a moment when Mark came to see me.

'Go on, have a puff, mate,' he would say, heavy with persuasion. And eventually, I cracked. 'Give it here!' I cried, taking one good, long drag. And while I loved the immediate escapism it gave me, that longed-for relief, it was – oh, so temporary. I could have cursed myself, for I knew that, because of that one puff, I would struggle for the rest of my sentence.

Addiction has always been part of who I am. I was an all-in or all-out kind of guy. Now I was back in bed with the weed, and it wasn't long before I too fell into debt. I scored a puff or two each day plus one in the evening. At £5 a smoke it got very expensive, very quickly.

I became crafty at borrowing from different people and efficient at juggling who I paid off and when. But this method was a struggle and created a lot of tension. It was especially tough on canteen days but I somehow managed to keep most people sweet.

Your reputation in prison is everything. And the stronger you appear, mentally and physically, the more you are looked up to and able to handle your own affairs. It was the best way to get through on the inside. Unfortunately, my reputation was going downhill fast. The deeper I got into debt the worse things became for me.

The running for fitness stopped, as did the meditation. I also halted my spiritual reading. But I didn't neglect attending weekly chapel – mostly, I must admit, because this was the only way I could get an extra phone call home. The smoking cycle continued for some months, wearing me down. It also hit my immune system, putting me in prison hospital for days with chicken pox.

This actually came as a relief, as I was at least able to rest for a while.

I had few visitors in prison. It was mainly my mum, who has always stuck by me through thick and thin. Another was David, my Christian friend, whose visits were especially welcome as he brought me the news that three hundred people from his church were praying for me. That was so heartening. Just the thought that so many people, unknown to me, would take time to pray for me, made a deep impression.

As the time for the parole board interview came ever closer, I became more and more anxious. On the day itself, I showered and put on some clean and well-pressed prison clothes, before heading off to the meeting.

There were three people interviewing me: two men and a woman. And I felt I had answered their questions reasonably well. 'Do you think you have been rehabilitated during your sentence?' enquired the rather stern-looking woman from the bench.

'Oh, yes!' I replied convincingly. 'I made a terrible mistake, and I am really sorry. Since coming into prison, I have gone to chapel regularly, I have been baptized as well as doing some running to get fit. Now I'm ready to go home and make something of my life.' I didn't think it helpful to mention my most recent past, or the fact I was back to smoking cannabis and owed a lot of money to a lot of prisoners.

'Thank you very much, Simon. We will make our decision and let you know within two weeks,' she said by way of dismissal. The interview, and with it my chance of an early release, was over. I would either be free in a matter of weeks, or face the hideous thought that I could be serving another year. The pressure was on once again.

How was I to get through the next two weeks before I found out about their decision? Prison time drags by naturally. Now each day seemed like a lifetime. Mark and I did a lot of smoking over the waiting time. Eventually decision day dawned, and the letter arrived. Officer Jones came into the dormitory waving the envelope that would shape my next few months. 'Williams,' he shouted, 'I think you've been waiting for this!' I tried to read his face, wondering if he knew the contents already. Time seemed to slow even further, my heart beating harder.

'Go on, open it,' instructed Mark, as others crowded around us. Parole decisions provided a great source of excitement to all prisoners. My hands shook as I took hold of the envelope and pulled out the all-important yet flimsy paper. My heart thudded and the voices around me became muffled. Slowly, almost reluctantly, I went to read the letter as sweat ran from my forehead. Suddenly, I was aware of feeling really sick. Dare I read it?

'Come on, get on with it!' cried Mark and others, including Officer Jones.

'OK, OK,' I blurted out, almost in tears. In the next few moments, you could have heard a pin drop as I unfolded the single page to read the verdict: 'Parole Approved'. I threw the precious paper in the air in celebration. I could hardly believe it! All the pent-up emotion was released as the tension drained away and elation took over. Unbelievably, I was going home in six weeks' time.

10

Freedom

My first thoughts were for my mum and, as soon as I could, I read her the good news over the phone. In addition, I was entitled to some short home leave within the next two weeks – a standard prison procedure to re-acclimatize prisoners to the outside world.

As expected, Mum was ecstatic and started making plans for my homecoming. Once I felt calm enough, I started to make plans for leaving myself. There was a problem, of course. I still owed an awful lot of smoke money to an awful lot of people. Somehow, to survive, I had to find a way of repaying what I owed.

Having tossed and turned throughout the night, there seemed little choice but to resort to smuggling in cannabis in order to pay off my debts. This was very risky, but no alternative came to mind. Home leave was always on a Friday and, as my weekend came around, I got very excited. Nine long months had gone by since I had seen the outside world. Now the prison door was opening – albeit just for the weekend – and I breathed in a taste of the freedom to come. Wonderful as it was, it did not solve my indebtedness problem.

The two days at home were tense. I spent most of my time arranging a delivery of cannabis sufficient to repay all that I owed. I would need at least three quarters of an ounce – then worth about £75 but priceless in prison – to get square. Happily, I was able to make contact with an old friend and, even though I had no money, he accepted my promise that I would pay him back when back on the outside.

Once I had been supplied, I had to manipulate the stash in the microwave oven in order to shape it like a bullet. This would have to be inserted internally to get it past the guards on the prison gate. It would be uncomfortable and risky, but it would solve my problem.

Monday morning came around all too quickly. Having wrapped the dope up well in cling film – and with the help of some Vaseline – I was able, with some effort, to insert the bullet internally. All I had to do now was return to prison and pray I wouldn't be too thoroughly checked over. As I approached the prison gates at 9 a.m., I started to panic, fear gripping me. My whole longed-for parole was on the line. The consequences if I got caught were as dire as not repaying the prisoners I owed.

Ringing the bell for entry, I tried to calm myself. I took deep breaths and tried to relax. Not too much of course, complete relaxation might mean an early release of the cargo I carried. As the large metal doors swung open, I was pleased to see Officer Jones was on duty. Of all the guards, I got on best with Officer Jones.

'Good morning, Williams,' I heard him ask. 'How was the home leave?'

'Fantastic, thanks, guv. Lovely to be back though,' I quipped, trying to lighten the mood.

Jones laughed. 'OK, here are your prison clothes, strip off your civvies and put them in the box.'

I was really hoping he wouldn't strip-search me; they didn't always do that. Putting my prison uniform back on quickly, I shouted: 'OK, guv, all done.'

'Right, Williams, step forward and open your arms wide.'

My heart jumped as I tried not to think of the cannabis stowed inside me, or the desperate involuntary loosening of all I held. Clenching my buttocks, I put everything I had into keeping things chatty, calm and – crucially – contained. It wasn't easy, especially when Jones started patting me down. Distraction was called for.

'Busy weekend, guv?' I enquired, keeping him talking.

'Same old, same old,' he answered. Then, to my huge relief, he opened the door to my dormitory, saying, 'Off you go then – and keep out of trouble.'

The relief of getting through the search was overwhelming. But I'd made it, and once I had 'unloaded' I would be able to pay back all those I owed. There were just two weeks of my sentence left and then this particular nightmare would be over. Yet strangely I was getting nervous of being released. For all its faults, prison for me, and for many prisoners, provides a place of security. It's somewhere to sleep plus three meals a day – guaranteed. Many men come back inside time and again as they can't cope with the outside world.

Release day in February 1991 finally came around. I woke early and gathered my letters and belongings together, then set off to say goodbye to those who had shared my life over the last months.

I admit my emotions were mixed, and although happy and relieved this part of my life was over, there was the nervous challenge of starting over again. There was no doubt in my mind at this stage that I had learned my lesson. The past few years had been enough adventure for any man. I was resolved to make something of myself and never to enter prison again. Ridding myself of my addiction, however, would take much more commitment.

Good old Officer Jones was on the release hatch again. 'Don't come back, Williams,' he called.

'Don't you worry, guv,' I answered. 'I definitely won't.'

With that, Jones finally opened up those enormous iron gates and I crossed through. I had heard somewhere that, if you look back, you're bound to end up going back. So to make quite sure, I kept my eyes looking firmly ahead.

My good pal, Sam, was there to collect me, having driven 50 miles to take me home. It was so good to see him. I got in his car and immediately felt immense relief. The nightmare was finally over, and I found I was breathing more easily as Sam set off, stereo at full blast with all the latest songs.

Slowly, I entered the real world again. The sights and sounds formed a pathway back into normality. It was a eureka moment. I didn't make any promises to myself, I didn't look back on my time in prison. I just enjoyed the sense of relief and release that surrounded me. There would be time enough to make the big decisions and new self-promises. Once more I just relaxed into the moment. And this time without the aid of substances.

Sam dropped me off at home where Mum was waiting, with the biggest smile on her face. We hugged each other, both of us weeping with sheer joy. 'Surely now, Si,' she pleaded, 'you'll settle down having learned your lesson?' There's nothing more forgiving – or more optimistic – than a mother's love.

Once on the outside and with plenty of time to think, I started to ponder on doing something worthwhile. After all, even at the best of times it's not easy to find employers ready to take on someone with a prison record. In any case, I wasn't ready to think about work in the conventional sense.

It was voluntary work that really appealed to me. Perhaps it harped back to the call I had years ago to go and work in India.

For some unknown reason, I had kept up my correspondence with Stella throughout my prison term and she strongly predicted that, looking to the future, I would work in a hospital. What she also told me was that, at some point along the line, it was there I would meet my future wife.

The idea of settling down with a wife and family of my own struck a chord with me. It was about time I came to rest, especially after all the travelling, the adventures and hazards I'd come through. Slippers and fireside had definite appeal. Looking back now I realize it was more the concept that I was in love with but, even so, I was completely taken in by Stella's psychic prophecy.

The next few months were tough as I adjusted to 'normal' life again. I met up with many old friends and we took up many of our old ways. I continued to smoke cannabis but sensibly never went near dealing again. All too soon, I found I was getting bored by the monotonous routine and wanted to get away from what I considered the ordinary. My easily addicted heart was, as always, focused on the extraordinary. So my mind turned back to exploring volunteering and trying to match it with Stella's hospital prediction. Realistically, however, I still had months of my parole to complete and that would limit any far-fetched plans I could dream up.

I was at least free to float some of my volunteering ideas again so I applied to a company, and I was offered a position caring for a young man called Patrick with cerebral palsy, living in Andover. This would certainly get me away from the many temptations lying in wait in Suffolk, and I also thought that this might give me a chance to put something back into society, rather than take it out. I hoped, too, that it might vindicate the long list of bad choices I had made. I still hadn't reached a full understanding of forgiveness or the method by which it can be achieved. But that would come in time. I had after all found some degree of faith in prison chapel. I had been baptized, even if I still hadn't grasped what the implications would be for the rest of my life.

By now it was 1992, and although I got on really well with Patrick, I was also getting quite lonely. Patrick was getting more and more independent, living in his own flat and driving a car. My job was to help him with things like cooking and shopping as well as addressing his personal needs, such as getting washed and dressed. We went for long walks together, sometimes taking a drive in his car and ending up at a local pub for a meal. But I was essentially friendless, being so far from my usual gang of pals.

I had heard on the grapevine that my friend, Val, was now living in Cornwall with his new girlfriend. It wasn't that far away, so I decided it was high time I went to visit him. Mobile phones then weren't the fixture they are today. So, with no landline contact, I had to take a chance on him being at home when I called in unannounced.

Andover to Porthreath, I discovered, is about 200 miles. But always the optimist, I reckoned I could hitch a ride and be there in about five hours. Hitch-hiking was still pretty common in the nineties, its dangers not widely recognized until some years later. My weekend off came around and I was free from Friday to Monday – an ideal time for a visit. My plan was to stay over with Val, and hitch-hike a ride back, ready for work on Monday morning. However, as with so many of my plans, things didn't quite go the way I intended.

That Friday evening, I soon realized there were fewer cars on the road than I had expected. Those that did stop only took me a few miles along my route. It was getting dark, and it began to dawn on me there would soon be fewer than ever cars coming along my way. Nothing for it but to make for the nearest village for an overnight stop. There, I found a disused barn just off the road. In addition to the increasing darkness, it was getting cold.

It was then I spotted an unoccupied pick-up truck nearby, loaded with firewood. It didn't take me long to redirect a few logs and get a good fire going before snuggling down in my sleeping bag for the night, warm as toast. Just before closing my eyes, I couldn't stop the thought that once again, as on so many of my ill-conceived trips, something or someone somewhere was looking after me.

The next day however, didn't help my progress much and it took until Saturday evening before I finally reached Porthreath. Locating the address, which turned out to be a beautiful chalet set on a hill overlooking the beach, I knocked on the door. It was opened by Val's very surprised girlfriend, Sarah. Sadly, she told me, Val had taken the coach back home for the weekend and wouldn't be back until Monday. The full irony of this was that we had probably passed each other on the road!

But Sarah was fine about my stopping over for the night. She was having a few friends over for the evening to indulge in some magic mushrooms, and I was invited. Although I was shattered from the journey, the addict in me could find no resistance to the pull of a druggie party. I was in.

Magic mushrooms were everywhere in Cornwall at that time. The many lush, green meadows were strewn with hippies and ravers, all ardently picking them. As her guests arrived, and as a special treat, Sarah made some very strong mushroom tea. This would help the evening go with a swing, she told me. Sadly, the 'swing' wasn't to include me. To begin with I hated the taste, not unexpected as this was seriously potent stuff. But the pull was there, and I soon settled in, becoming excited about the trip I was about to take.

It didn't take long before I started to feel the full effects. This was confirmed when I noticed the newscaster on BBC was speaking in a Mickey Mouse voice. Colours started to fade in and out and I felt small vibrations and electric shocks in my head. Not long after this, I descended into a bad trip – a really bad trip. I soon became panicky and just wanted it to end. At one stage the mushrooms were actually speaking to me! They were threatening me, saying that if I ever invaded their territory again – they wouldn't let me out! I knew I had to get out from under their spell. And fast.

Luckily, Sarah had the answer in the form of some vitamin C tablets which, she promised, would help to stabilize me. Eventually, the mushrooms and their devastating effects started to fade, and I fell into a deep sleep. It was a horrible, unforgettable experience. I remember promising those demons I would never 'invade' their territory or go near them again. I did though, and only ever once more. My dad had warned me of the lifestyle I was leading and called it the 'Twilight Zone'.

The last time I ever did mushrooms was when I was leaning on a fruit machine in a pub and I turned round, bedazzled with all the lights on the machine. I looked at the name of it and it was called the 'Twilight Zone'! I immediately let out a scream and shouted, 'My dad was right!' It must have turned a few heads in the pub that night.

Early on Sunday morning, I was back on the road. I couldn't wait to be away from there. Soon, I was hitching and praying for someone to pick me up and get me at least a little nearer to my destination. Again, I experienced that amazing feeling of luck – or was it provision – of something or someone taking care of me as a driver stopped within minutes, and to my joy was going all the way to Andover.

I arrived back at Patrick's house still suffering from the effects of the bad trip plus the exhaustion of the journey. Once settled in, I saw among Patrick's prescribed medication, some Valium tablets and, having taken them before, I knew they would help my hungover state. So without Patrick's permission, I took one. But as ever, I couldn't stop at one and went on to take three more. This inevitably started a big row as by now I was slurring my words. Patrick was furious and called in his medical team. The volunteering team were the next to be called and I was fired immediately.

Despite all the good things that had happened to me, despite the feeling I was blessed in some way, despite believing I was being cared for – I had fallen, and hard, yet again. There was nothing else to do but to return home to face my mum and try to explain how I had completely blown this opportunity.

While trying to appear pleased to see me, I could see the despair in her eyes. Sadness was written in her face and as she tried to hold back her tears, she quietly asked: 'What will you do now, Si?'

'I'll look for another voluntary job,' I answered brightly, knowing full well that gaining another job with my record would prove very hard indeed. I was haunted – and I would like to think by now, thoroughly shamed – by the pain in my mother's face. She fought so hard to hide her disappointment and worry. At last, I took time to think about all I had put her through over the years. But those thoughts were still held captive to the 'quick fix' and the buoyancy of my misplaced optimism.

I thought back to all that Stella had predicted, about working in a hospital and meeting my future wife there. So without too much thought, the very next day I contacted my local hospital and, to my amazement, they offered me a voluntary job in an old people's home. This was great news as I was able to start the following week. It turned out to be very demanding, but I really enjoyed it, making many new friends.

Two weeks in and still enjoying the work, I saw a pretty girl walk through the ward, looking as if she too worked there. We glanced sideways at each other and before long we were talking to each other. There was an instant attraction, and it wasn't long before I was asking Becky out for a drink. I half-believed that this was living out Stella's prophecy.

As time ticked by, our relationship continued to grow; we had much in common with our jobs and I felt comfortable in her company. However, behind the scenes, I was once again in contact with Mac who was, at this time, organizing more Acid House parties. Mac still loved the party scene although, like me, he had vowed never to deal again. In no time I was beginning to help him out, which meant I had money in my pocket for the first time in ages and it did seem, to me at least, as if I was in control until, that is, we linked up with a group of guys from London with a reputation for holding highly successful raves, in Cambridge.

For me, things felt as though they were going well. I had a little money to play with as the raves were doing well. I was doing my voluntary work and I had a pretty girlfriend. Crazily, I continued to smoke cannabis and also acquired a taste for cocaine – the preferred drug on the rave scene then. But it wasn't long before the raves started to attract all the wrong kind of people. The hardline, criminal element soon got involved and things turned sour very quickly. It was uncomfortable, even dangerous, and I wanted a way out. It wouldn't be easy, there's no sentimentality in those guys, and leaving the group and their working arrangements was hard. You couldn't just say, 'Thanks for the opportunity but now I'm off!' It just didn't work like that. I needed an excuse to get out, a good and convincing one. And it wasn't long before I got one.

My relationship with Becky was still going strong. We enjoyed each other's company and I really believed she was 'the one' that Stella had promised all those months ago. Becky also had her own place and so it was easy for us to drive home together at the end of our shifts. Soon I was living there and, before long, we could genuinely be called an 'item'. Things really were looking up. I felt as if I had reached a place where I could be happy.

One evening I arrived home to find Becky standing in the hallway waiting for me. Her expression did not bode well. Something serious was up. I had never been that confident around women, having been ditched at least a couple of times before. For all my bravado and unshakeable optimism, I always felt nervous around the opposite sex. I immediately thought this was it – she was bringing our relationship to an end. Her expression almost shouted 'it's over' at me. I broke out in a cold sweat as I waited. But then again, I recalled that Stella had said I would marry my encounter from the hospital.

'Sit down,' Becky demanded briskly. 'I have something to tell you.'

I waited, shaking, then she said: 'I'm pregnant.'

The room went cold and very quiet. I was so relieved that I wasn't being dumped that I let out a sigh of relief. Then started laughing. Was it that the words hadn't properly sunk in? We just sat staring at each other for quite a while.

'How do you feel about that, then?' I asked her.

'How do *you* feel about it?' she countered.

'I think it's great,' I said, and to my surprise I realized I meant it.

'Really?' she said, now with a big smile on her face.

The ice was broken, we were both delighted. Hugging each other, we collapsed on the sofa to discuss the future, full of baby talk. It felt so right, and Stella's prediction looked all the more solid. We had met in hospital, and we were attracted to each other. Now there was a baby on the way. What more could I ask for?

For a while, things went well for us. We rented a new, larger house way out in the country, surrounded by green fields and lots of quiet. We were set on making a go of it, for the baby's sake. Living together did present unplanned stresses and strains, but we did our best to get along as we prepared for the new arrival, despite neither of us being properly prepared for parenthood.

In 1993 my son was born safe and well. By then, I had quit the Acid House party scene and I'd got a proper job, selling PVC cladding. While it was reasonably well paid, it certainly wasn't enough to build a career on. It also meant drumming up business door-to-door, which was stressful at the best of times.

It's a well-known fact that all new babies produce considerable tiredness and tension. I suppose a lot depends on how well you are prepared for it. Neither of us were. So, sadly, after ten months of living closely together, Becky and I realized it just wasn't working for either of us. Was it due to us carrying too much baggage from the past, or maybe our expectations were too high? Whatever the reason, it was obvious this relationship was going nowhere. For everyone's sake, especially for my little boy, we mutually agreed to part. And to my lifelong sadness and regret, I wasn't to see my son again for many years.

Once again, I had no feasible choice but to return to the family home. Although Mum made me welcome, it was a hammer blow to the dream she had of me settling down into family life. For me, the promised vision of slippers and fireside had juddered to a halt. I had tried to make it work but it seemed that, for me, this was one dream too far. With a lot of sadness inside, it wasn't long before I was spiralling down into smoking cannabis and endlessly partying yet again. All I wanted was to tranquillize the pain of parting from Becky and my son. I wanted to hide from the waste my life had been so far. At that point, I knew no other way of living with myself, or admitting to my bad choices. Cannabis was my comfort blanket. You could wrap yourself in it and become invisible; you could blank out everything that hurt. The only thing it couldn't do was clear the path to a happy, more fulfilling life. How couldn't I see that?

But life goes on, and it wasn't that long before I met Gayle. She was a pretty girl, full of fun, and soon we were good friends. Better still, she was on her way to Ibiza to work for the 1994 summer season and asked me to go with her. I wasn't doing much at the time and got quite excited at the thought of visiting the party island.

I felt sure of finding some new work for myself alongside a playboy lifestyle. Good fun as Gayle was, there was disappointment waiting for me on arrival in Ibiza. Time, money and job opportunities ran out – fast. The only thing left to keep myself fed was selling time-shares, mainly to Germans. I soon became very uncomfortable with this. While not exactly conning people, as they got all that they paid for, there was a lot of trickery in the selling methods. Our job was to get clients sufficiently interested to tuck them into a taxi, which took them to where the 'hard-selling' professionals would finish the job. Ironically, for all my drug-taking and petty crimes, selling time-shares did not sit well with me at all.

Fortunately, I had kept in touch with Val throughout the summer and, once he had finished a painting job (yes, he really did go back to painting and decorating), he planned to come out to Ibiza to join me. I was really looking forward to seeing my old friend, especially as the short-lived relationship with Gayle was fast coming to an end.

Val arrived with some cash on him, which was always welcome. However, this was destined to last us barely a week. We were getting off our heads most nights with a delicious mix of cannabis, LSD and cocaine. But it all proved very costly, and money once more became a problem. We tried small jobs ranging from working in a beach bar to DJ-ing. But our attempts at playing our guitars to entertain bar customers came close to a fight with the owner one night. Clearly this was not the way forward.

With the relationship between Gayle and me now over, Val and I decided to travel to Ibiza old town, to meet yet another friend, Colin, who had come out for a couple of weeks. It was good seeing old friends and getting together again. But as funds began trickling away, we were forced to make new plans: to travel to mainland Spain. The real attraction was that Val's mum and dad had a villa in Torrevieja.

We scraped just about enough for the fares to get to Denia and then planned to travel by bus to Alicante, and from there on to the family villa, around 100 miles away. We said our goodbyes to Colin and hopped on a ferry. I wasn't in a good place at that time. I hadn't had the chance to wash my clothes properly for weeks and the aroma was not very pleasant. My skin was dry and flaky, and I was in really poor shape. Two months in Ibiza – with little money, few amenities, and no decent food or jobs – had taken its toll. But things were going to get better, surely?

Val had already spoken to his mum back in the UK about us going to her villa and we were full of excitement as we arrived in Torrevieja. Val's mum had arranged for us to collect some money from her on-site cleaner, Beryl, who looked after the apartment. What we didn't realize, however, was that we were still some miles away. We had next to nothing and there were still some hot, dusty miles between us and the villa.

'Let's get a taxi and hope Beryl, plus the money, will be there when we arrive,' was my suggestion.

'What if it's not?' asked a concerned Val.

We were both exhausted and hungry and needed to get there soon as night was on its way. In the end, we plumped for the taxi and, after Val had given the driver the address, we settled down comfortably for the last few miles. Once we arrived, Val went off in search of Beryl and the promised money. He was gone for some time. The taxi-driver was getting very anxious as I crouched down in my seat, trying to be invisible. 'Come on Val,' I breathed. I was really at the end of my tether. Happily, he came back with a delighted smile, holding the taxi fare aloft. What a relief!

Money and keys were supplied by Beryl; we climbed up to the apartment. 'Wow!' I remember thinking, taken aback with the cool luxury inside. It had everything we could want – including a much-needed washing machine. There were fresh towels, and lovely comfy beds. Better still, there was also a shop where the San Miguel was on special offer. It both looked and felt like a mini-paradise. Once again, I sensed a little bit of heaven had opened up just for me. What a contrast to the last couple of months.

Val and I spent two wonderful weeks there. We enjoyed constant sunshine, a dream of a swimming-pool and the relaxation that comes with the holiday atmosphere. I couldn't help asking myself, what had I done to deserve this? How do I keep landing on my feet? Why do I feel this strange sensation that, despite the bad choices, dishonesty, and the ill use of so many people, somebody, somewhere is showering me with good fortune?

The lazy, hazy days were passing by all too quickly. I felt I was back in recovery mode. Perhaps that someone tasked with taking care of me was slowly but surely putting me back together. We ate and swam and relaxed.

A lot of attractive women in bikinis were in the area, distracting us both. There were families too, all enjoying their well-earned summer break. It made me think of my son and, for a brief moment, I wondered what it would be like to holiday as a family unit.

And then the next extraordinary thing happened. Toward the end of our time there, two very attractive girls came to stay in an apartment within the complex. Not slow to make new friends or miss an opportunity, I soon got talking to them and we became quite friendly. During the course of conversation, one of them told me how she used to baby-sit a little boy. It didn't take long to realize it was my son she was talking about. I was full of questions. How was he, what was he doing? To begin with I felt sure this was some sort of sign that I should go back and renew my relationship with the little boy. But, yet again, to my eternal regret, I let that moment pass. Once again, I was ignoring the signs that were so clearly laid out for me. I will never know what the damage of ignoring that sudden prompt would mean for either of us. Had I listened and taken action, it might have changed both our lives.

As it was, our time in the apartment was up. Reluctantly, we handed back the keys and made our way back to the UK.

11

Settling Down

It was now 1994 and I settled back home at my parents' house again and looked for a job, to try to finally find some normality in my life. It was back in Bury that I finally met my wife-to-be. This, of course, heavily contradicted Stella's earlier prediction, that I would meet her in a hospital ward. She had obviously got it all wrong because – although I found Suzanne in the place where she worked right enough – it was at the local job centre, and very far from a hospital setting.

I was immediately attracted to her. She was slightly built and had an extraordinary air of calm about her. Her friendliness, smile and unhurried manner were totally alien to me. It was a classic case of opposites being drawn to each other. She was, in my eyes, beautiful, and I fell completely in love with her. I realized I had never felt this way before. Five years younger than me, my immediate thoughts were that Suzanne was right out of my league and way above my pay grade. But I had fallen for her hook, line and sinker. Love doesn't listen to reason.

During our long, easy conversations together, Suzanne told me she had been brought up in a Christian home and went to church as a child. She wasn't interested in things religious now but, nevertheless, all that she learned and believed in would eventually come back to sustain her in later years. And not only her.

She had just come home after spending some months in India where, through a voluntary youth scheme, she had worked at Mother Teresa's orphanage in Calcutta (now Kolkata). Perhaps it was there she had acquired that quiet stillness which I found so irresistible – a patience I would come to rely on so much.

Soon, I left Mum's house and, together with Suzanne, moved into a rented static home, on the outskirts of town. Life was good for both of us. We jogged along really well as a couple and discovered we shared a love of travel and adventure. It didn't take us long, however, to discover that settling down in the conventional sense just wasn't for us. Our conversations were well-peppered with potential travels and planning a future full of exploits abroad.

At that time, I had got a good job at the local sugar beet factory where I was working hard on a campaign which was bringing in some serious money. I actually found myself saving! Extraordinary! I was changing, accepting this new trace of domesticity and it felt good. But the old travel bug doesn't lie dormant for long and, fortunately, that was true for us both. We lived modestly, deciding to save and go travelling together once I had completed my contract.

The campaign finished in February 1995 and by some miracle – and under Suzanne's influence – we had saved enough to go to our dream location in Thailand. I had also been giving some thought to my son, and wondered how he was faring. Happily, I had heard on good authority that he was doing well and thriving within a stable family setting. Becky now had a steady partner and as a family they were happy. All things considered, I couldn't compete with that, and I decided things were best left as they were. To be honest, I was still susceptible to the odd smoke, but fortunately things hadn't spiralled down any further.

Suzanne and I flew off to Thailand in late February and stayed in the Khaosan Road in Bangkok for five days before heading south on an overnight bus to Koh Samui. The place was incredible, full of rich sights and sounds plus some wonderful people. We both loved it instantly.

Happy as I was, I had never quite got over my paranoia of losing out on long-term relationships. I had been let down so much in the past and by now Suzanne was becoming ever more precious to me. I didn't want it to end. Continually smoking weed did not help my fears but Suzanne was always there, coaxing me out from under the black cloud of insecurity. I liked to think we made the perfect travelling companions. And I hoped that this time, we would go the full course.

We travelled to Koh Phangan, then on to Koh Tao. The love affair we both had with Thailand seemed perfect; how could it not? The bungalows were rented from just £1 a night. The beaches were fantastic, as if straight out of a holiday brochure. The food, too, was out of this world. I couldn't help wondering why I had never thought of coming here before. What might my life have been like if I had chosen Thailand over Israel?

Together we explored the islands on a rented motorbike, and I realized I had never felt such peace and freedom in my life. The smell of burning coconuts as we drove through the densely forested groves, plus the aroma of fresh seafood from the street vendors, was totally intoxicating.

Our days started with coffee and me smoking a spliff, enjoyed in a gently swaying hammock overlooking the beach. Across the horizon was a group of other islands, each one looking equally inviting. A good curry for lunch was finished off with a cooling swim in the truly blue waters. In the evening, a few Singha beers were washed down with a delicious local speciality. And all of it readily available for just a few pounds. It was idyllic, if only we could have stopped the clock and just stayed as we were for ever.

Sometimes, Suzanne and I would walk inland, where we admired the lifestyle of the local monks. We would watch them most mornings as they walked around the village, holding out their begging bowls for alms. We discovered, too, that the locals who donated them various foods were supplying the only means by which they ate each day. The fact that those monks were so calm and colourful stirred something up in me. I would look at them and remember some of my own spiritual journeying. While most of the time I had been stoned, I did recall a small voice of reason niggling away at me. And I couldn't help thinking that, as happy as I was, I wasn't yet

on the right spiritual track. Those tranquil monks, however, making their way around their villages for a handful
of food, impressed me deeply. But life was just too good
for further meditation.

Hugely reluctant to leave this heavenly place, we nevertheless caught a bus for Bangkok, keen to miss none of
the sights and landmarks that country had to offer. From
there, we took another overnight bus to Chiang Mai, in
the north of Thailand.

On arrival, it didn't take us long to sense that this area
was nowhere near as beautiful as our southern haven.
There was less excitement around and less fun too. Not
surprisingly, it didn't recommend itself to either of us.
Strange really, because it was right here, in this spot, that
something significant was about to happen for both Suzanne and myself.

My curiosity surrounding the monks, their constant presence and their Buddhist way of life, continued
to draw them to me. I had, some time back, looked at
Buddhism in my long delve into things spiritual. For a
while, in my prison cell, Buddhism had captured me. It
appeared uncomplicated and sensible, gentle too, and certainly worthy of further exploration. But afterwards, as so
often happens with the addled mind, I simply lost interest
in anything that required either deep thinking or sacrifice.

One of the main tourist sites in Chiang Mai was the
wonderful Chiang Mai temple, called Wat Phra That Doi
Suthep, so named for the mountain on which it was built
in 1382. We both climbed the three hundred steps to
reach the base of the temple, where the views were beyond

magnificent. We just stood there in awe and amazement, incredibly moved and lost for words at the beauty.

Half an hour later, having explored the rest of the site, we realized how tired we were from the long climb. Happily, we found a bench and gratefully collapsed on it while recovering our breath. Directly in front of us, about 20 yards away, was a huge glass container bulging with local money. We couldn't help staring as people fed it with yet more. Standing beside it was a woman dressed all in white. For some reason, my eyes locked into hers and I was overwhelmed with a deep, almost physical sense of sadness. It was as if time was standing still; I was transfixed, unable to explain why I was looking at this mysterious woman.

As she looked directly into my eyes, I knew instantly that there was a reason behind our encounter. From inside me came a prompting, an inner voice, and it was telling me plainly that this was not the way I was meant to go, or even be. This temple, the money – the Buddhist faith – this was not for me. Right there and then, I felt so strongly that I should allow it no place in my thoughts.

To this day, I wonder if I had seen a warning angel? Was there something deeply meaningful in the message I was receiving? All I knew for certain was, angel or not, this was a serious, even life-changing message. The temple, for all its beauty, was and is something I must put behind me. I felt I was treading the wrong spiritual path, looking in the wrong direction.

The message and inner voice would not be easily dismissed. As Suzanne and I got back to our hostel I shared my experience with her. We discovered that for some un-explained and uncomfortable reason, we had an urgent need to find a Christian church. So early next morning, we got on our moped and drove around the town looking for one. It didn't take long to find and, better still, it was wide open. We parked the bike and made for the door.

As we went inside, we heard the sounds of a choir, practising. It was so beautiful, almost unearthly, so we sat, stunned, at the back to listen. Once again, I was overcome with emotion – this time with elation. It was incredible, listening as the angelic voices washed over us. We sat, mesmerized, for some time – just listening and absorbing the beauty of voices praising God. Instantly, I knew what I was going to do the minute I returned home.

I was realizing that only a great God could have stepped into the chaos that was my life. Only a great God could have provided for me, cared for and rescued me, from the life-threatening situations I had put myself in. Only a loving God could have prepared the countless escape routes I'd been offered, for sure. The same person had saved me from almost certain abandonment and ruin. There had to be a different purpose for my life. But how to find it?

I knew I had been delivered many times. There had been many signs, especially when – for the briefest of moments – I realized that happiness is not found in cheat-ing and recklessness. I used to say I believed in God – but did I really? I also used to say God would have to speak to me loud and clear to get my attention. But hadn't he done just that? Hadn't he always been there through the dangers and near misses? How many more proofs of his amazing love did I need? It was time to listen; a time to feel shame – a time to transform, by leaving my old habits behind and starting over again. As ever, Suzanne, while not quite in the same place as I was, was nevertheless hugely supportive.

But as ever, life calls us back to cold reality. What treasure do we miss by not following the guidelines and inner promptings? What opportunities do we miss along the way?

The experience surrounding the visit to the temple in Chiang Mai would resonate with me again, a year or so later. I had kept in touch with another long-standing school friend, known as Quinny. I had always had an interest in his travels, following his journeys around the world. So I knew that, at that time, he was in Thailand.

Under some compulsion, I wrote to him and told him the story of recent events and our strange encounter at the temple. Perhaps I was still looking for some meaning from the experience. I wrote the letter to him and did not have time to write the envelope, so I asked Suzanne to do that for me. Quinny was able to pick up his mail from the Bangkok post office, and one day collected about fourteen letters and began by reading the ones he recognized first. Over the next two days, he travelled up to Chiang Mai and opened the letters as he went. Having not recognized the handwriting on my envelope, it was one of the last he opened. In the letter I recounted the spiritual experience I'd had in the temple. He later recounted that he was totally blown away, as he was sitting in the very same temple when he read it.

Our blissful and revealing time in Thailand inevitably came to an end. But Suzanne and I had come back to the UK with new resolve, our lessons, memories and experiences not forgotten but stored away, within easy reach. We rented a picturesque country cottage on the outskirts of town, and I got a job as a delivery driver while making finding a church my first priority.

We settled on a community church not far from where we lived. The vicar, Jonathan, was friendly and accessible. He recommended me to the Alpha course – a worldwide, question-friendly video course, running in more than one hundred countries and in many different languages. Twenty-four million others have done this course, many of them finding its contents to be life-changing.

While Suzanne had no personal interest in all I was doing, she continued to encourage me to go along to meetings. Even though I loved the church and the acceptance and encouragement I received there, there was still very little real change in me. My propensity to smoke cannabis continued. I tried so hard to give it up but couldn't get a breakthrough. I also loved my tobacco cigarettes too.

Suzanne and I made some really good friends at church, and they would stay friends for many years, each one having a profound influence on my life. Martin and Erica became great friends and are still to this day. Martin and I have shared many godly moments and he has always been a great mentor and spiritual brother.

I became enveloped in the Bible, which led me to believe that Suzanne and I should get married. Our relationship had to become permanent and lasting, and it had to be in line with what the Bible taught. We were living together, and I knew that was not God's way. Suzanne didn't share the same belief at this time but happily said yes when I proposed. And so we got married in our local village church, in 1996. Our first beautiful daughter, Hollie, was born two years later, with Harry and Ruby to follow over the years. All are wonderful children whom I love dearly and have been a source of joy to us both.

As we settled into parenthood, church gradually became more of an on-and-off thing. I was still smoking a lot of dope and my insecurities and paranoia, around women particularly, continued. I made occasional trips to church to say sorry for my weaknesses but found it impossible to break the habits. I would give up for a while – then go right back to them. The longest I could stop was one month at a time. It was a frustrating and lonely path, and I was disappointing myself at the lack of progress.

Significantly, Suzanne, now happily settled, decided to take some further education, choosing a history degree at the local college. It was for that reason we bought our first computer. While Suzanne found it useful for her studies, I found it totally compelling and became absolutely fascinated with 'why and how' it worked.

Five years into our marriage, we decided to get into the property market and moved closer to town, buying our first house. This was quite an achievement for someone as restless as I used to be. I was still a delivery driver at this point but my fascination with computers grew and, when an opportunity – sponsored by a government grant scheme – arose to study computers, I jumped at it. Along with friend Colin (who had been with Val and me briefly in Ibiza), I enrolled for a six-week course in Cheshire, with a guaranteed job offer at the end – or you could reclaim your money. It seemed to be too good to be true but both Colin and I walked straight into jobs at the successful conclusion of the course.

My job entailed moving around Suffolk and Norfolk, fixing hardware faults. It came with a company car, and I found I loved the job I was doing.

Sadly, however, I was still horribly stuck in a round of drug-taking and it was getting worse again. Whether it was due to stress or weakness I don't know, but I developed a dangerous taste for cocaine again, which inevitably caused havoc – if not at work, then certainly at home.

I started to go out most weekends and, before long, I had begun on-line gambling; another ultimately addictive and destructive habit. My mind seemed to be split in two halves and I just couldn't break free from what I knew was so very wrong. I loved my growing family dearly. But then I also loved going into that drug-fuelled nowhere land and forgetting everything else. It was causing huge tensions within the marriage, and ever-patient Suzanne was stretched almost beyond her limit. I tried to blame it on the pressures of work, being a husband and father plus my domestic responsibilities. But deep down I knew that *I* was causing the destruction, and that my behaviour was set to destroy me and my family.

The quick fix I sought had me going to church to seek some sort of forgiveness – real or imagined. Then, almost immediately, I found myself going straight back to my wrong ways, superficial forgiveness forgotten. Words don't impress God – actions do.

There were many rows at home and by now Suzanne was getting depressed. This must have had an impact on Hollie as children are usually very receptive to what is going on in the home. The most formative years of a child's life are generally the first seven, and Hollie was around that age at this time. I always quote the saying now: 'Show me the child 'til they are seven and I will show you the adult.' I later learned that through God's healing and forgiveness, these early years could be healed.

Suzanne was also expecting our second child. Once Harry was born, I vowed again to be a good father and to quit the smoking and gambling. Again, although I meant it at the time, it proved an impossible task. My resolve lasted such a short time before I was back to my old ways. Somehow, I was able to hold onto my job and my house although, with constant borrowed financial top-ups, the mortgage was getting bigger by the day. I was using anything and everything to keep up the payments, but somewhere and somehow it had to end.

What was I thinking? While I had acknowledged God in my life, I wasn't following him, and I certainly wasn't pleasing him. My constant plea for forgiveness meant nothing without following it through. It was so easy to slip back into the same, selfish groove. I might hold my head in my hands in anguish, but that was indulgence. I hated myself so much that when temptation beckoned I didn't – or couldn't – ignore it.

Strains within the home were becoming unbearable, especially for Suzanne, but it was telling on the children too. My Bible, now collecting dust, wasn't offering a solution and I was getting desperate. A crisis was coming but, as always, my solution had to be bigger and larger than life – and twice as risky.

At the height of this misery, I had a call from old friend Quinny. He was off travelling again and this time his destination was to be Dharamsala, India, where the Dalai Lama lives and teaches. I was beyond desperate by now, just wanting my life to change. In my heart, I wanted to be a good father and husband, but all those good intentions couldn't stand up against the lure of the dope I was used to.

Once again, I was regretting my neglect of my son, who I hadn't seen for some years. And now there was the very sad but real possibility of a marriage breakdown. It was all too much for me. I decided Christianity was clearly not working – at least not for me. It was time to go and check out all that Buddhism stuff again and see what it had to offer. Quinny was offering me a trip to see and hear the Dalai Lama. It seemed a sensible step to my addled mind. Perhaps he could solve my sorry state. And so I deliberately chose to forget those former warnings. There had to be an easier way.

Looking back, I cannot marry that kind of thinking with the truth which I had acknowledged just a few years earlier. Where was my gratitude when God stepped in to rescue me from foreign prisons and dangerous minefields? How easy it is to blame God when life goes sour. How hard to see the love of God in tough times.

Suzanne was really pleased when I said I was going. Any break or rest from me and our failing marriage was such a relief for her.

After a long flight, Delhi proved a big culture shock for me. The streets were filthy, the mass of people oppressive, the noise of traffic deafening. Even though I had been warned about it before flying, I found the reality almost unbearable. First there was the utter chaos of navigating my way out of the airport. Then the sad sight and sounds of the many beggars lining the streets. Crowding in on me were the deafening shouts of warring taxi drivers plus the stifling heat too.

I had to make my way across Delhi and find the bus station where I would board an overnight bus to Dharam-shala. That long, intense journey took twenty hours be-fore I saw, to my utter relief, my old friend waiting for me.

I slept for what seemed like an age and woke look-ing forward to seeing and learning from the Dalai Lama's teaching, tuning in for translation on an FM radio. The place was buzzing from the huge crowd of different peo-ple gathered there to listen. They ranged from monks and devotees to thousands of travellers, like me. The hot walk up from the dusty road to the temple was filled with street vendors. The smells from the food stalls, the in-cense, and the fresh smell of being in the foothills of the Himalayas was a very sweet aroma.

On entering the temple, I found it strange – and a bit chilling – to see the security guards were well-armed with guns. It didn't take long before I discovered, sadly, that I just couldn't engage with the mystical teaching on offer. All I was aware of was my urgent need to find the good, strong dope that I had heard was readily available in India. And it wasn't long before I came across just such a supply. It turned out to be the strongest stuff I had ever smoked.

Good as it was, it had its price, as from this point on I became very ill and had trouble breathing. Every time I took a smoke, I would gasp violently for air. I actually thought I had contracted severe asthma. Fortunately, I found a chemist and bought myself an inhaler which helped for a while. But the relief didn't last long, and panic began to settle in. It was a terrifying experience. I tried stopping smoking and relaxing. Just to be sure, I also bought some Valium to see how that worked. (You could buy just about anything in India.)

We left Dharamsala and headed to an ashram near Rishikesh. The journey was very beautiful but also quite unnerving; we took a taxi through the foothills with mind-boggling drops off the edges of cliffs. Around some corners we could even see smashed-up vehicles, mainly buses, in the ravines below that had not made it. This did not help the fear that I was already experiencing. I did not enjoy the ashram experience much either.

Because I was still very unwell, Quinny and I decided I should go back home to the UK early. This whole experience clearly was not for me. But as always God was working in the background, as I would later understand, to bring good out of the mess that I felt myself in.

Propped up by the Valium, I managed to get my original flight changed and headed back to Delhi. On arrival, I found a hotel to rest in. I was becoming more and more ill. Panic was taking hold of me big time. On top of my symptoms, I realized I was suffering from the obligatory 'Delhi belly', due to carelessly eating some suspect food from the train. And just to top off the nightmare, I discovered my hotel room had a blocked toilet!

By now, I dared not smoke. It just aided the panic I was feeling. I felt I was dying, and my stomach was aching badly. I did still have some of the dope and, stupidly, I hid little bits in my tobacco pouches, so I could take some home to England. The two days in Delhi prior to my flight home just couldn't go quickly enough for me. On the day of my flight, I ordered a taxi and got to the airport in a haze. As bad decisions go, this Indian trip was probably the worst yet.

I was completely off my head on Valium as I walked through the airport. This eased the panic and fear that I was feeling, but must have looked very suspect to the security guards as I went through the gates. If they had found the dope in my tobacco, I could quite easily have ended up in an Indian prison for ten years or so. I am grateful this was not the case; I boarded the Virgin flight and, happily, I was able to sleep soundly all the way home.

12

A Second Chance

To be home again came as the biggest relief ever. It was so good to see Suzanne and the children. But there were problems. The drug that I had relied on so heavily throughout my many ups and downs was now causing panic attacks every time I took it. (There was an obvious message here, of course.) I sought the advice of my doctor, who promptly prescribed more Valium. However, that was tougher than I expected; I hated taking the tablets as they made me very drowsy and extremely irritable the next day.

There began a war inside me – a rage of feelings I didn't understand. Next came my reaching for the temporary, artificial calm of Valium. Slowly, I began to realize I had buried so many emotions over the years. Now, many of them were rearing their heads, jostling for position and control of my life.

I began to dwell on the neglect of my dad for being away at sea for so much of my childhood. It had all played such a negative part in mine and Andrew's upbringing. I chose to identify this as a major cause of my problems – especially those times he could have come home but chose to go drinking instead.

The fact I hadn't seen my first-born son since he was a baby was yet another issue that I had got used to pushing down into my unconscious. It was so much easier to bury those bad feelings with on-line gambling and long sessions at the local pub. I was not a big drinker and I liked to think I could hold my ale well. After all, two pints were known to cheer me up no end. But somewhere, behind this semi-rationality, lay the heavy dependence I had now developed on cocaine.

It was so easily available but, at £50 a gram, cocaine certainly wasn't cheap. My indulgence in late nights, gambling, drinking and taking cocaine turned into a race to find money to feed my habits. So I continued borrowing against the ever-increasing mortgage. Life at home too, was stretched almost beyond limit. Now she was pregnant once again, with our third child, I sensed my relationship with Suzanne was at breaking-point. I believed she was planning a separation. When Ruby was born in 2005, my habits and morale were at rock bottom.

Possibly from a sense of desperation and shame, I took to staying out longer and longer at night. At the same time, money to sustain my lifestyle was getting a daily – almost hourly – challenge. Often, after coming down from a cocaine high, I would use the weekend to break down, to cry or have a panic attack. In those moments I would promise Suzanne I would go back to church, I would repent, ask for forgiveness and I would change. Even to me it sounded hollow, as I was on a never-ending cycle. There was no way this could end well. Within days all my promises would be off the table, and I would be right back to where I started.

But where exactly was I? Who was I? What was wrong with me?

Among all the evils I was caught up in, I realize now I had lost all sense of my moral compass. I had descended into a world of drink, drugs, gambling and lust. I had abused the love and trust of my lovely wife and broken the heart of a good mother. Yet I hadn't started out like this. I couldn't blame a father's absence for the depths I had sunk into or the unhappiness I had showered on those who loved me. I was drowning, I needed rescue and I knew that only something truly dramatic would achieve it.

By now I was 39 years old. I was completely frustrated and totally out of control, especially when it came to indulging in binges. Arguments and unhappiness were swirling about me – and yet somewhere in the far reaches of my mind I was aware of a secret promise, one I believed God had made to me. I was sure he had promised to deliver me when I was 40. I had read so much of the number 40 in the Bible that I hung on to being delivered at that age – when Noah builds the ark it rains for 40 days and nights; the Israelites were delivered out of Egypt and wandered the desert for 40 years; Jesus was tempted in the wilderness for 40 days. So 40 seemed to hold something very miraculous to me.

Amazingly, during all this turmoil, I was holding down my job as a mobile computer engineer. The trouble was I had an awful lot of spare time on my hands as jobs were few and far between. How I used that time could go either way. Happily, I was to spend much of it with my new church friend, Neil. He would try to guide me and prayed for me constantly. It was during these times I met yet another Christian guy, Mike, who was to help me make the right moves. An ex-paratrooper, Mike invited me to his church, and a new phase was at last opening up for me. Later, much later, I would laugh to think that God had sent the paras in to pull me out of a difficult spot.

Despite a complicated medical history, Mike had set up a charity – Aid to Hospitals Worldwide (A2HW) – that sent refurbished medical equipment, for free, to the developing world. He relied heavily on volunteers to accomplish this and, to me, this was an obvious choice for filling the gap between jobs and downtime. I stepped in to help where I could.

At its heart A2HW was Christian, and I found myself working alongside a great number of people who shared Mike's vision, and his faith. It opened my eyes to see that Christianity wasn't just a way of thinking but a way of working too. There were retired craftsmen, technical guys, administrators, packers and warehouse operatives, all offering time and talent for free to help others. Among them was a group of vulnerable adults with learning disabilities. Looking back, I can see how many of these guys' limitations would, in another context, also fit me. I too was caught with fewer options in life, but for me it was due to my imprisoning habits.

As Mike and I got to know each other over the next few months, it became apparent to him that I was leading a double life. He sensed too, that I was in quite a bit of trouble mentally and emotionally, reasoning that it was this that was causing my destructive ways. While I helped his charity where I could, life for those at home was getting bleaker. Hanging over me was the knowledge that Suzanne was preparing to leave me. It just wasn't fair to the children. I shared this with Mike, who decided to pray and wait for God to make a breakthrough.

I still couldn't stop taking drugs and by the time my fortieth birthday came around, there seemed no end to my misery. I was in deep despair at what I was doing. But no matter the agony, I just couldn't help myself. I was drowning.

A few weeks passed and I was still chained to my old habits. One day, however, after scoring my usual first gram of coke, I decided to go uptown to meet some friends. The buzz that cocaine produces had changed for me by now; it had become a burden – there was no joy to be found in it anymore. This particular evening I stood at the bar, gazing wide-eyed at those on the dance floor. All of a sudden, I experienced a devastating wave of loneliness. I finished my drink quickly and started to walk home. Negative thoughts were crowding my head and a total desperation overcame me. What was the point of carrying on this life of mine? It was all so pointless.

I had never had thoughts like this before. I had come to the end of myself, and I just didn't want to carry on. Thoughts of Suzanne and the kids flooded my mind. What a terrible waste my life was. The more I thought, the more sadness overwhelmed me. Then, ten minutes from home, I suddenly experienced fierce anger welling up inside me. I was angry with everyone – with God, with my dad but, most of all, with me. As anger turned back to sadness, I felt something stirring deep down, perhaps to my very soul. Then, an almighty cry came out of me: 'God, save me from this! I can't take anymore!' As soon as I let that cry out, I felt something in me snap – somehow, I had changed.

Later Mike would quote, 'It is at the lowest ebb that the tide turns.' It is so true. Sometimes a person has to get to the end of themselves before they can be helped; and we can only be helped when we really commit to the help on offer. It's a lesson I have never forgotten.

Next day at A2HW, Mike wished me a cheery 'good morning'. But it took him only seconds to realize I was crying helplessly. With Mike's arm around my shoulders, we went into his office where he prayed deeply into my whole life situation.

One of Mike's God-given gifts is the ability to sense any troubling presence of evil in a person. He knew at once I needed deliverance from a demonic presence – a release from the spirits that had bound up my life. 'Exorcism!' I shrieked when Mike suggested it. The very thought was abhorrent and chilled me to the bone. Carefully, Mike explained that what I needed was the help of a specially trained and ordained minister to displace the evil influences that clung to me.

An Anglican priest, experienced in this special ministry, was found. My circumstances were explained to him and, because he was assured I truly wanted to take this step, he was keen to help me. Through calling on the name of Jesus and being truly sorry, he explained,

I could rid myself of the satanic grip that had plagued me for so long. Nothing short of complete surrender to an almighty God would achieve the change in my life I so desperately wanted.

And so it was agreed that together with Mike, my local pastor and the Anglican priest, I would pray and petition God to release me from my demons. A date in June was set. Until then, I had to stay strong and prayerful. Did this really mean an end to my failed attempts to live the sort of life I wanted? I wondered. What would it be like to be free from the compulsion of drugs?

A few weeks ahead of my deliverance date, Mike asked me to compile a list of all the things that I regretted in my life. It was a long list. This time I was profoundly convicted of the length and breadth of the disasters and wrong turnings that had punctuated my life. It went far deeper and was so much more meaningful than my preparation for baptism in Norwich Prison.

As May started sliding towards June, I became very unsettled. I found it hard to think of anything other than my forthcoming exorcism. I was more and more convicted of the sin I had allowed to dominate my life, and I was weighed down by the battle going on inside. I didn't know it then, but when Satan senses he is losing his hold on a life, his demons fight to keep his place. Were the energy surges from when I was practising chakra meditation perhaps a demon or demons getting hold of me? These were all thoughts going through my mind.

The tension caused by my overwhelming anxiety culminated in an episode played out at my brother's wedding.

Dad, Mum and I flew out to France where Andrew and his wife-to-be were to tie the knot. Two nights before the ceremony, we had a big family meal together where a lot of alcohol was consumed. In my tense mood – and to my horror – I became abusive and rude, finding all kinds of reasons to cause havoc. Such was the heat of the moment, it escalated into an ugly fight.

The whole family showed their utter disgust at my behaviour, and they insisted I fly home early. I was devastated. How could I have ruined this happy occasion for those I loved? Suddenly, I found myself welcoming my release from the demonic, now just days away. I concentrated hard on the list I had been asked to make, recording all the wrong things I had done and now hated myself for. I was ready now and longing for some release.

On that June morning, I woke up and quickly lit a cigarette to accompany my strong coffee. Suzanne was still very sceptical of what was to happen. She had heard so much of my boasts and promises in the past, she had little reason to believe this was for real.

On arrival at the church, I found the other three were waiting for me. We sat around a table on which a single candle was lit.

'How are you feeling?' I was asked.

'Nervous,' I replied truthfully, clutching the long list of sins I had prepared. To my great relief that ugly list, composed of all that I had hated about my life, was taken and ceremonially burned, unread.

There followed a great deal of prayer and petition, the Anglican priest calling on Satan to leave me, in the name of Jesus Christ. I looked around anxiously at their faces. I wasn't feeling anything special happening. Was that it? Next, I was called to pray for my own deliverance, to cast out the evil that had taken hold of me for so long. Scripture was quoted to remind me that the place once occupied by Satan was now emptied (Matt. 12:43). I had to fill it with Jesus and his Holy Spirit. At that moment, I vowed I would never allow anyone but Jesus to own or occupy any part of me.

Back down to earth, I returned home to a still-doubting Suzanne. Was it real? Had that really worked? Had it really happened? Was I truly changed? Questions flew through my mind.

Two days later, still reeling from my experience and looking for some inward sign, I spotted that Trinidad and Tobago were playing football against England in the World Cup. It looked good, so I went to the local pub to catch the match with some friends. Maybe it was the general atmosphere or a simple lapse, but after a couple of beers I found myself longing for cocaine. I quickly found some, it was all too easy to obtain. I wasn't thinking straight – I had the urge and here was the means!

I returned to my table and took the cocaine. Then I saw a man sitting in front of me, the back of his T-shirt stretched tight across his shoulders. In horror I stared at the image imprinted on it. There in front of me was a large and vivid picture of the devil, its eyes staring back at me. All of a sudden, I started sweating; my breathing felt constricted, coming only in short bursts. I felt God was showing me – rescuing me – just before I fell back into the drug trap. With that clear sign, I got the confirmation that something fundamental really had changed. Right there and then, I was moved to pray a quick prayer of remorse – genuinely sorry for my actions. Now, I knew for sure that all that had happened was real; God had heard my cry and led me – yet again – into a place of safety.

I gave up smoking within a few weeks. Every illegal piece of music was wiped off my PC. I had been warned by my Christian friends that the next few months would be tough. But I wasn't going to be alone in this new life. God was healing and mending my heart and walking with me. It was up to me to reject what I knew was so wrong. It wasn't going to be easy – but then it isn't meant to be.

I slowly began distancing myself from my old friends. Somehow, I had to move my family away from the estate and its pub where so much temptation still lurked. But moving our family, now we were five, was not that easily done. So I prayed. I asked God to enable us to move to a new place, where we could make a fresh start. In trust we put our house on the market and it was sold to the first person to view it. Incredibly, her name was Miss Gold!

Next, we found a nice house in a village ten miles out of town and began to build our lives back together again. We immersed ourselves into church, where we felt at home and made many friends. By now, Suzanne was beginning to see a huge change in me, which pulled her back to church. It wasn't always plain sailing, however, and I struggled many times, but then Mike was always there on hand to pray and reassure me.

Suzanne was embracing this new life and we found ourselves enjoying the Bible and other Christian reading together. Slowly Suzanne was accepting the new me and relishing the way we were rebuilding our family. One day, Suzanne saw something of God's care for herself. She was in a Christian bookshop and picked up *The Bondage Breaker* by Neil Anderson.[3] As she read the synopsis, she knew at once this book would be helpful for me. Looking at the price, however, she realized she didn't have enough on her. We were struggling with money at that time.

The next shop she visited was a charity shop and, browsing the shelves there, she saw the very same book for a fraction of the cost in the bookshop. She had to take a second look before uttering a 'Wow! What were the chances of that?' Further down her own Christian walk, Suzanne would know for herself, that all things – big and small – are possible with God.

The book was indeed a revelation. It explained how harmful habits, negative thinking and irrational feelings all lead to sinful behaviour that can keep a person in bondage. It goes on to assure the reader that if they feel trapped by any of these strongholds, they are not alone. They can break free. The author has brought hope to millions who face similar attacks, through a book that offers a holistic approach to spiritual warfare, according to Scripture.

For us, the next steps came quickly. Having seen the change in me, Suzanne too gave her life into the keeping of Jesus. Both of us were baptized in our new church – exactly two years to the week after my escape from bondage. What an amazing and special day it was as we both got baptized by full immersion and fully accepted Jesus Christ into our lives, by stating that we believed he died for our sins and rose again on the third day, and that we would serve him for the rest of our lives. We knew God had a plan for our lives and though there would be challenges and disappointments along the way, we felt confident that the worst was behind us, and we had a new future to look forward to. This was completely different from me getting baptized in Norwich Prison, as back then I had no real conviction of my sins even though I did believe. This time I was fully aware of my sinful nature and my personal need of a wonderful, loving, forgiving Saviour in Jesus.

13

New Life

It took a while to adjust my eyes from the bright sunlight outside to the gloom within. The walls were dark and the passageway where I stood was narrow and claustrophobic. I felt myself digging in my pocket to reach for and then to surrender my mobile phone. A crisply uniformed guard patted me down and directed me to the camera where a brief photo shot was taken. Nearby a none-too-friendly dog sniffed me up and down. All highly unnerving. As other doors swung open, there was that unmistakable stench of mass cooking — mainly cabbage. I felt my stomach lurch.

I was back in prison once again, the one place to which I had sworn I would never return. All at once the old fears and feelings came flooding back and I couldn't stop the shudder that ran down my spine.

As I stood with high, barbed-wire fences on all sides, I recalled the long journey that had led me here. I remembered the horror of being alone, the lure of drugs and those threatening relationships formed out of a common bond of powerlessness. It was as if I had been pulled back here by a force I didn't quite understand. It seemed life itself had contrived to push me back to where I was least comfortable. And most unhappy. *Gazing upwards, I experienced a crushing anxiety as I remembered those long, long days in the cells – dumped and forgotten in order that I repay society for my bad choices.*

Thank God, I whispered to no one in particular, that this time was quite different. I wasn't destined for the deep inside with many years of confinement ahead. This time, I was here by invitation, on a mission to bring a little light into the darkest of places.

I was nervous, of course. My incarceration wasn't that far back in time. Memories, as unwanted as they were, bore down heavily. But things were very different now, I reminded myself. Now, there was a great weight of expectation on my shoulders, not least from myself. It had been quite a journey to get here, and I sensed both the joy and the burden of many hopes and prayers surrounding this venture.

I turned and smiled at the guard as he respectfully ushered me and my companions into a side room where tea and biscuits were on offer. I was treated with great courtesy and some curiosity because, this time, I was here at the invitation of the governor himself. I was here to share the peace and hope I had found in living a different way.

I felt that this was the path I was meant to tread – an opportunity God had created for me, not just a payback for so many wrong turnings, but a purposeful start to the rest of my life.

I couldn't help wondering how many of us get such a chance.

But first things first. For some time I had known, deep down, there was a new pathway I needed to take and a still, small voice I needed to heed. There was also a wealth of temptation to ignore. But where and how to start?

Since my conversion, life in general had been good. It produced its challenges and strange turns of course but, if asked how I was feeling, I would have to say my days were lighter and so much more rewarding. I was filled with the Holy Spirit, which made me feel more joyous, more peaceful. I didn't feel alone anymore. I felt the love of the Lord in my heart and felt the love of fellow Christians. I felt I now belonged to a wonderful new family. It was like someone had turned a light on inside me and I could see the light of Jesus shining all around me. I was now thinking differently and more coherently; I saw where my sin had been in my actions and my thinking and now the new path was clear in my mind.

My work took me out on the road, answering calls for computer help over a wide area. There were days when these calls were frantic and others much quieter. This gave me time to continue my work with A2HW, which was opening a whole new world to me. I enjoyed meeting other Christians who devoted long hours to serving God in practical ways. They were there to help people they would never see or meet, yet there was so much enthusiasm for all they were doing. The day job was paying well, and my home life was running smoothly. Temptations were still there but resistance was getting easier. My eyes were wide open to the Christian world now, how it worked as well as how it felt. And it felt good.

One day, Mike told me that the A2HW charity needed to get a consignment of restored bicycles over to Germany. A very welcome task. I asked a good Christian friend called Brian to help me, and we decided to make a weekend of it. Our recipient was a Christian mission ship, sailing under the banner of Operation Mobilization. The ship was currently docked in Kiel where, once the bikes had been unloaded, they would help the ships' crew travel around when arriving in foreign ports. We picked a date and travelled down to Felixstowe, to take a ship for Holland and then on to Germany.

The ship we were aiming for was the *Logos Hope*, which travelled to scores of different countries around the world, its floating libraries bursting with Christian books to give away at the many ports it visited. Perhaps it was there, among those millions of words, written in so many languages, I developed a longing to write my own story. Not for profit or glory, but in order to tell others how a life, no matter how shattered, can be turned around. I wanted everyone to know that a life lived with Jesus can bring an amazing transformation.

We met up with Graham, who was from our hometown and would later become a good friend, and pastor of my local church.

Our journey took us to the ship's berth, and we were welcomed aboard and taken on a trip to meet the two-hundred-plus multinational crew, made up from dozens of countries. Each crew member brought their own special skill to the benefit of the company. Duties were assigned accordingly, with engineers, chefs, teachers, musicians, cleaners and many more in between. You couldn't help but be inspired by their dedication, hard work and big Christian hearts.

Exciting as it all was, I was still suffering from periodic panic attacks and always at the worst times. Despite the friendliness and relaxed surroundings, I began to feel an attack coming on, made much worse because I was so far from home. But I shouldn't have worried because help was at hand.

The resident pastor aboard called some friends together and, laying hands on me, they prayed that I would recover quickly. In addition, they prayed for a permanent cure – one that meant these disabling attacks would never again cripple me and tie me up in knots. Receiving their prayers helped me to cope almost instantly. From that time on, the fear and panic of those attacks were banished for good. Not for the first time, I was left wondering at God's healing power and how vital prayer was. It was a powerful reminder.

Once back home again, it was through experiencing the ups and downs of family plus the inevitable petty squabbles, that I began to realize we were both still carrying a great deal of emotional baggage. Never a good thing. We both recognized that our past lives were casting big shadows across our futures. We needed to deal, once and for all, with all that had gone before in order to fully enjoy what was ahead. So we were excited to hear about a Christian healing centre, in Sussex, that could help us shed this load.

A little gingerly, we took the journey to the centre, not sure what to expect. On arrival, however, we soon experienced a peaceful presence in which to enjoy what was to be a revealing weekend. The programme was well-structured, our days consisting of healing, meditation and personal prayer, plus ministry time. This consisted of sharing some of my life with a couple of people, who were then able to help, advise and pray with me. In between, there were delicious meals and good company to enjoy.

As I sat quietly on my own in the centre's chapel, I gazed up at the father-figure backdrop of Jesus. This was a wonderful painting of Jesus' face, and his eyes just gripped me straightaway; I felt a real connection with him. Almost immediately I experienced an overwhelming sense of being loved. Through tears, I sought God's help in forgiving my dad for his many absences and neglect. After all, I could understand his lifelong battle with the bottle so much better now. In those stilled minutes, I was able to let go the frustrations and hurts alcohol had caused us. There and then, I promised God that, on my return home, I would tell Dad how much I loved him. Remarkably, once this promise was kept, we had a dramatically changed relationship for the rest of Dad's life.

As for me, I felt liberated. It was like a huge burden – one I had carried for so long – was lifted from me. Content for now, I experienced the comfort of knowing this was a place where I could face the weight of unfinished business with God – and resolve it.

My second visit to this tranquil centre some months later had the same life-changing effect on me. As before, it was an emotional visit and this time God clearly showed me the cause of another inner turmoil. He revealed it arose from guilt at abandoning my baby son all those years earlier. While I knew God is willing to forgive those sins we freely admit, I was beginning to understand that one of the most difficult acts we face in a Christian life is forgiving ourselves.

I could do nothing about my past, yet I was constantly berating myself for letting my son down. On my knees, I wept tears of shame. Would God ever help me repair the damage I had caused? It wouldn't be easy, I knew. After all, he was a man now, and I had no idea how to find him.

My prayer was for a reconciliation – a chance to ask my son's forgiveness. I knew I had to find him for answers, no matter how long or painful the journey.

That second visit also produced an equally strong message for Suzanne. She too, felt God's presence surrounding her, and God healed her of some of the burdens she had picked up during her lifetime.

A third visit was also an emotional time of healing for me. I had always been quite untrusting of women, especially in relationships, and would often find myself paranoid, thinking they would like other men more and run off with them. This was particularly pronounced in the days when I used to smoke cannabis and would suffer from many paranoid delusions.

I phoned Suzanne up to tell her about my day at the healing centre and, when she did not answer, I immediately felt gripped with paranoia about where she might be. It was more intense than normal. I cried out to the Lord for help, and he immediately took my mind back to when I was about 7 years old. My dad was, as usual, away at sea, and Gan, seeing the distress and loneliness in my mum's life, had organised a blind date for her. I remembered Mum getting ready and the man waiting in his car outside. I begged Mum not to go. All I remember wanting at that age was for Mum and Dad to be happy and to be together. The Lord showed me that this was where my distrust of women started. I have long since spoken to Mum over this. She too hated the date, and it never happened again.

I don't blame her now, nor Gan, as the loneliness and trauma when my dad came home in those early days must have been terrible for Mum. It does go to show, though, how things can have an effect on a small child. It amazes me that when the Lord illuminates something like this in a person's life, it can be like a light turned on, and they can see where something began and, in turn, the healing of it can then be started.

However, it doesn't take long to travel from the heights of a godly encounter right back down to everyday life! While I was amazed at all the new things I was learning, life ticked on and soon it was back to everyday work for me.

Inside I knew this new way of living was gradually changing me. Spending quiet times in prayer first thing in the morning anchored all I did during the day. I developed a real hunger for reading the Bible, amazed at how relevant it is for today. It gave me truth to hang onto when challenges arose. I made a habit of metaphorically 'wearing' the 'sword of the Spirit' (see Eph. 6:17) – which is God's word – every day. This Scripture talks of the armour of God and how we can use it to resist the devil. After all, Jesus made a habit of living by the words of God, his Father, imprinting them on his mind and heart. He used them regularly to resist temptation. Yes, even Jesus knew what it was like to be tempted.

One morning I found myself in my car some way from home, answering a call for technical help. I had woken up that day feeling decidedly down, a bit oppressed and low. I was so tempted to have a cigarette. It was worrying too, for this temporary unwarranted gloom could so easily have overwhelmed me. What to do? I decided to pull over and, once I came to a halt, I pulled out the laminated sheet I always carry with me. On it I had written some Bible verses. I made myself focus on reading them out loud, as I found reading out loud to myself really helped my still fragile belief. I calmed right down.

God really showed me that day the power of his word and how we can use it to make the devil flee. I started to call aloud the truths of who I am from the Bible. As I was shouting these out, a car sped past me, screaming up the road ahead. But what caught my eye was the number plate – it read '666', the sign of the devil! Strangely, instead of feeling panicked, I felt relief. I recognized that God was showing me the danger I was in – and the devil had raced away from me by me using the sword of the Spirit which is the word of God (Eph. 6:10–17). I then realized the power of Scripture and how Jesus used it to get the devil to flee from him after his forty days in the wilderness.

It wouldn't be the last time I experienced such a sign. Some time later, I would actually lead a Freedom in Christ course, which stemmed from the Neil Anderson books. I was especially anxious the first night I was due to lead it, as I had not done anything like this before. Suddenly on the way to the meeting, a car was going slowly in the outside lane just in front of me. As I looked at the number plate, I noticed it read '666'. I immediately thought of my previous encounter and said calmly, 'In the name of Jesus Christ of Nazareth, move out of my way.' The car immediately pulled over. A calm came over me once again and I was assured that God was with me, as ever.

Of course, I am aware that these and other happenings could easily be shrugged off as mere coincidences. But for me, taking Jesus into my everyday life has been rewarded by a sense of his presence in *everything* I do. Nothing is ever wasted with God, and that includes our very smallest experiences. He doesn't just know, he cares too. It's an awesome yet wonderful thought to know that, when temptation comes, you're not fighting it alone. There's always someone overwhelmingly mighty in your corner. There's a wonderful verse in Isaiah 46:4 which really speaks to me: 'I will be your God throughout your lifetime – until your hair is white with age. I made you, and I will care for you. I will carry you along and save you' (NLT).

I believe God works in our lives even when we don't know him, and he pursues us throughout our lifetime, urging us to change direction and come into fellowship with him, to enjoy the wonderful life that he offers. I don't think today that God was ever aiding me in my life of crime and wrongdoing, but I believe he was pursuing me to bring me back to him and certainly to save me from near death on a few occasions. I think we will always reap the consequences of our sin and wrongdoing, and we are not immune from that, but I truly believe that God never forsakes us even when we are apart from him.

It was rewarding to find that among the rush of home, family and work life, my circle of friends was ever-widening. I decided early on that I wouldn't try to hide my past. It is a risky strategy in a biased and judgemental world. But in the end, I came to feel respected for my openness. It meant the friendships offered were genuine and honest. There was never the dread that someone might 'discover' something in my past, something I had tried to hide. So I accepted the risk. I knew some might condemn me, view me differently, even mistrust me. But God's goodness to me is something I wanted to share. He deserved the recognition.

It is nevertheless a tough decision to make. I ran the risk of being eyed with suspicion, even losing friendships. But weighed against the stress of carrying secrets, I decided that, for me, it was better to be open.

After much thought and prayer, I decided this truth-telling should include my almost adult children. Admitting to your own drug-taking, when your kids stand on the doorstep of adolescence, is not easy. It removes the right to moralize and opens wide a case for them to use it against you. However, in seeking God's guidance first, I found a way to gradually uncover what I had done and who I had been, while leaving it to them to judge who I was now.

All three of them were regularly attending church and enjoying the teaching and friendships made there. Forgiveness, like starting over, was not a new concept to them. But then neither was the background of drug-taking and addiction.

Small facts had come out regularly during the course of family life. So, nothing was too much for them to handle gradually. But still, I was their dad. Would this alter our relationship? For me, honestly revealing my past mistakes – and that included a prison sentence alongside addiction – gave me the freedom to demonstrate God's transforming influence on my life. While there was little applause, to my relief, I felt there was no condemnation either.

Some months later, I was introduced to a very interesting couple, Richard and his wife, Gipsy. We seemed to hit it off straightaway and, during the course of conversation, they told me about their involvement in a prison-based ministry. My ears pricked up immediately. I had already felt an urgency to give something back for all the good things that were happening to me. My new-found faith was beckoning me towards serving God in some way, although I had no idea how that would play out.

Richard talked to me about his work with Kairos Prison Ministry – an international, Christian-based organization which aims to address the spiritual needs of imprisoned men and women while also supporting their families. Through a series of talks, prayer and meditation, over five designated days, Kairos presents the love and forgiveness found in Jesus. It also presents the hope of a future to even the longest-serving prisoner.

Kairos course activities are run by a specially selected and diverse group of trained volunteers, who spend time with the prisoners over the course of a week. Widely used in the USA, Kairos had sadly been stopped for some years in Britain, possibly due to a lack of volunteers.

Richard was now keen to start them up again and he had applied to lead a course in one of the region's Category A prisons, housing those with many varied sentences. Kairos obeys the call of Matthew 25:36, which says: 'I was sick, and you cared for me. I was in prison, and you visited me' (NLT).

The whole concept struck a chord with me, and I couldn't wait to see how I could get involved. Having applied and been accepted for training, I discovered the next Kairos session was due to take place later in the year. There were still a number of training days to go before that could happen. I launched myself into training, enjoying every minute.

Based on Richard's belief that I would make a good team member, I began to look forward to the challenge of putting my learning into practice. However, there was one big worry and potential stumbling-block. I had a record. How would that play out with the authorities? Would my past scupper all that I was hoping would be a big part of my future?

I loved the whole concept of Kairos; if only it had been available to me while I was in Norwich Prison. I just couldn't wait to get involved. I had soaked up all the training and yet there was this constant worry that at the last call, because of my record, I might be barred.

On the last training day, Richard handed out prison volunteer application forms, urging us to get them filled in quickly as clearance – essentially the prison governor's permission – could take some time. My heart sank.

'I have a problem here,' I admitted to Richard, really upset and worried. 'When they look at my past, I may not get clearance at all.'

Ever the optimist, Richard tried to reassure me. 'That was quite a few years ago now, so it should be OK,' he shrugged. And with this, he collected the completed forms and we prepared for the long wait until getting clearance.

Would I get my chance to participate in this life-changing movement? I prayed so hard that I would.

During the next three months, while waiting anxiously, I met many new people. I joined the technical team at church, looking after sound and lighting, etc. as well as helping members with their domestic technical issues. However, the enemy was never far behind me, whispering negative thoughts in quiet times. Since my conversion, I had realized that I was in a battle of good versus evil. This was quite key for me as I had not understood that I was in this combat before. How can someone fight if they don't even know they are in a conflict? With my new-found knowledge and the help of the Holy Spirit and other Christians, I was able to begin to understand this, and muster up a defence against 'the fiery arrows of the devil' (Eph. 6:16), which the Bible tells us about.

Eventually the long-awaited prison clearance letter came through. It was not good news. I rushed to the phone to call Richard. 'Due to your adverse criminal record, we have not granted you clearance this time,' I quoted. 'I am so sorry, Richard. I have failed the clearance,' I told him.

'Don't worry,' he soothed. 'It may be we can get you in via the chaplain. Just write down your charges and send them to me urgently.'

Both Richard and I prayed about the outcome, again calling on God to open the doors for me. I felt so convinced this was what he wanted me to do. Surely when it came to prison experience, I reasoned, I had so much to give.

Even so, the full irony of this story was not lost on me. Here I was pleading so earnestly to get *into* prison when previously I had begged to be kept *out*!

Waiting was agony; however, the day came when my mobile phone started to buzz, and I could see the caller was Richard. I prayed it was good news. Cautiously, I answered to hear: 'Hi, Simon, Richard here.' He sounded chirpy, perhaps it was good news at last. 'It's great news,' he announced. 'I have heard back from the prison chaplain and the governor is going to let you in.'

Wow! I thought. God can even open prison doors for me!

Next came weeks of more nervous waiting for the date of my first mission. While my church pastor was very supportive, covering me in prayer for the task ahead, there was still this enemy voice whispering doubts in my ear, playing with my mind. Would I *really* be the help and guidance I hoped to be? Would God's presence *really* go with me? Could I *really* bring hope into the mess of these men's lives? The short answer is, of course, no, I couldn't. But I knew someone who could. The day of my first mission finally came around and I took the 50-mile journey to the prison with the team. Both men and women, my Kairos fellow workers represented quite a cross-section of society.

It felt very strange being back in prison, and I soon noticed a vast difference in the security arrangements. My old prison was nothing like as safety-conscious as the one I was now in. There were the X-ray machines, phone searches and finger-print scanners to get through before reaching the prisoners' quarters. The low growling and barking of large Alsatian dogs made the experience extra sinister. And it certainly didn't help my nerves.

Our accommodation for the week was provided by members of a local church and we were warmly welcomed by our host families. These good people provided our breakfast and evening meal while lunch was taken with the prisoners. Twenty-four male prisoners had booked in for the course, which was a good number.

The work began by the team putting out four tables for us and our candidates to group around. They were labelled: Matthew, Mark, Luke and John. Six prisoners and three of the team would sit around each one. There would be talks and discussions together with meditations and an opportunity to interact with others on their tables. Each man would be encouraged to take notes and even make posters as a way of communicating his thoughts. I, more than most, knew exactly how tough it would be in prison, to make public something so personal. There's very little that you can hide in prison.

The week would culminate in a forgiveness service on the Thursday, followed by a closing ceremony on Friday, to which we could invite our outside friends and family. On that first morning however, a closing ceremony seemed very far away.

All a little nervous but greatly excited, the Kairos team met in the chapel to pray prior to the work starting. As the prisoners filed in for the first time, we noticed they were a very mixed bunch. Each was dressed in prison-issue grey sweaters and jogging pants; some sported shaved heads while others had impressive beards. Easy to hide behind, I guessed. Some looked expectant, others fearful.

The one feature uniting them all were eyes filled with trepidation and suspicion. Each man was attempting a bravado he clearly didn't feel. Whatever had drawn them to apply – maybe the cookies we promised, the chance of getting out of their cells or possibly a genuine curiosity – nothing was offering them much comfort now.

As I greeted these men, I felt an inexplicable love for each one. I felt comfortable in their company. Striking up a conversation came totally naturally. Those first steps, which could have been so awkward, had a real easiness about them. After all, I had been here before. I had stood in their shoes and felt the same suspicion of new things they were clearly feeling now. Once again, I was struck by the way God never wastes our everyday experiences. So often he uses them to help us to relate to others. In this case, I was able to empathize with the prisoners in a meaningful way. For their part, I think the men felt and understood this too.

Over the next days we got to know each man really well. By the end of the week, most had been touched by the truth we brought them and were willing to talk about the new-found hope that was already making such a difference to their lives. This would be crucial to them in the following days. It was humbling to see grown men weep and be willing to share their thoughts with each other.

The men came from all walks of life, some from very troubled backgrounds and generations of dysfunction; some from very good homes, some with no fathers or mothers; some dragged up, beaten and abused. All had a story of some sort that really tugged at my heart. Nothing though that our Loving Father could not forgive or start to heal.

Before we realized it, the last day had crept up on us. We had reached our Friday closing ceremony and for this we would be joined by family and friends from home. By that last day, I had learned so much about so many of the men and their lives that it was heartbreaking to leave them.

All too soon, it was time for the closing ceremony. I had invited Mike and his wife, Ann, as my guests. Mike would always pray with me before I went into a prison and, many times, he had a special word for me. Sometimes that even included a name of someone I would meet. Being so connected even while we were so far away from one another made him a natural choice as a guest.

As the men filed into the chapel on the final day of my first Kairos week, I suddenly realized how emotionally drained I was. More than that, like others, I could see feelings were running high. Very soon we were going to leave behind the men we had got to know so well. How would they fare? We as a team would be praying for them, of course. But again, I knew from bitter experience that prison life – its routines, its rivalries and its constant temptations – would make it hard for them in the days to come. These men had become so special to us. Of all the team members, I alone knew the battles they would face to stay focused on Jesus in the coming days.

After the moving closing ceremony, during which hearts and minds had been laid bare, Mike and I joined the team to take tea with the prisoners. Tears were never far away. For us on the team there was the emotional relief of seeing friends, while for others it was the good-byes to come. Looking around, I saw I wasn't alone in feeling emotional. During the simple service, several of the prisoners had got up to speak and ask God's forgive-ness. They had also declared their newly placed trust. Such was their sincerity, there was barely a dry eye in the place – and that included the officers on duty. Did they recognize their need for genuine repentance too? And did they absorb the miracle God had worked?

We Kairos people all acknowledged it had been an amazing week, not just for the prisoners but for the whole team and especially for me. I had felt supernatu-rally empowered and immensely grateful for seeing how God moves. I had experienced his love for the men; his amazing way of reaching into their hearts to bring hope where before none could be found. No matter what any man or woman has done, God can and will forgive and transform any one of us when we accept his love for us.

I knew then that this was not going to be my last Kairos. As it turned out, it was the first of six, of which I had the privilege of leading the last. Each one was a unique blessing. The privilege of helping those who stood where once I had stood was humbling.

The whole experience hadn't been just for those prisoners. It had been for me and my team members too. It had impacted the governor, the officers and many others. Our faith had been strengthened and we saw how God loves even the least lovable. He had changed many of those men's lives and demonstrated to me there is no limit to what he can do – even through me, if I am willing. What a privilege. What a God!

The company I worked for every day had been incredibly good in allowing me time off to cover the prison work. I often wondered what motivated them to be so generous. Whatever the reason, it was a special blessing not just to me but many others too.

Keen as I was to enrol for the next – and then the next – Kairos visitation, no one had warned me I might be invited to lead one. What a responsibility. 'No way!' had been my instinctive answer. It made me anxious just thinking about it. But when Richard added his voice, I nervously accepted. I reasoned that, as three people had approached me about it, perhaps God was telling me something. Tense and worried, I realized I needed a lot of prayer support and preparation to equip me for this next challenge.

I would need a miracle to break into the prisoners' lives this time. God had provided us with many miracles at each Kairos event, including a rainbow over the prison when we arrived on one occasion. Another time we had been held up by one sheep on the road outside, which had reminded us of Jesus leaving the ninety-nine sheep to go and get the lost one. Above all, there had been the miracles of men finding forgiveness and giving their lives to God.

When I entered the prison, I quickly became aware of the sinister bleakness of the place. To calm my nerves, I reminded myself that Christ too was once a prisoner. So, despite my qualms, I thanked God there and then, not just for bringing us on another Kairos mission but also, as I believed, for equipping and empowering us to tell his story.

As on so many other Kairos journeys, we were to meet some unforgettable men during our week-long stay. Despite the strictness of the prison regime, we were able to reach into the lives of men whose earthly futures looked decidedly bleak. As ever, our reward was to hear more heartfelt confessions from those who had been transformed by meeting the living God.

No two Kairos courses are ever quite the same, as are no two men. But as always, the usual suspicion soon dissolves, and we came to be trusted by the men. It's always such a privilege to sit and listen – really listen – to a man whose spirit has been crushed and who sees little hope beyond the four walls in which he is confined. On this occasion, as on so many times, the days flew by, and

we came – all too quickly it seemed – to the emotionally charged closing ceremony. The team were tired and
drained, as was I. We had all felt the exhilaration of meeting with God as he offered the kind of forgiveness that
could be found nowhere else. But now, yet again, it was
time to leave.

Departure is always hard, but I knew before we left,
we would hear some heartfelt stories to pray over. As the
men assembled, we remembered again that Kairos isn't
just a collection of men on a course designed to help them
through prison life. Kairos can be a life-changing key to a
new life – one which prison walls cannot confine.

I couldn't have known it then, but my own circumstances were about to change, and this was going to be
my last Kairos closing ceremony for some time. While
every visit is unique and the list of those prayed for grows
ever-longer, this particular Friday closing ceremony was
to be very dear to me. On the surface, it was a typical – if
that's possible – ceremony, yet this particular one would
stay with me for a very long time.

As always, the men filed in to take their seats and re-
view the past few days. Thankfully, there are always some
who find the courage to stand and speak in front of the
invited audience that includes strangers, the prison officers, the governor and the chaplain. I wonder if anyone who has not been in prison has any idea what sort
of courage it takes to discard the bravado of prison life
to speak about your deepest feelings, to say nothing of
trusting in Jesus? But genuinely moved during a Kairos
week, as usual, there are brave souls who do, one often

spurring on the next. With little awkwardness and great feeling, they stood to thank God for the Kairos experience and the journey they were starting on.

The first man stood: 'Forty years ago, my life changed forever. I really thought it was over for me. Now I'm sixty-one and, after this week, I know it's just beginning.'

Encouraged by this frank confession, another stood: 'I thank God for bringing us on this Kairos journey. I was so terrified when I arrived here. Now I feel I am no longer alone.'

All of a sudden more men were standing, only too ready for their turn. 'I'm not very good at public speaking,' said one young man, 'but I'll regret it if I don't speak out. I genuinely don't feel I'm in prison when I'm here. I was heavily into spice, and it was killing me, so I prayed to God, and I haven't had a single urge to return to it.'

After a pause and almost timidly, a much older man blurted out: 'I'm right out of my comfort zone. I've been very depressed lately but, since I've come to Kairos, I feel like I've had a bit of life given back to me. Thank you, God.'

And then a final tear-filled voice spoke up: 'Something's calling in my heart and I'm pretty sure it's God.'

I knew then that if I ever got round to writing a book, I would want it to go first to those in prison.

As always, it had been a revealing week. Without the pervading sense of God's presence, these men would never have chosen to go to church, let alone take faith seriously. Like so many Kairos weeks, hope had been placed in hearts and minds previously so hopelessly lost – proof, if it were needed, that prison walls can't confine a man's soul.

Once again, the team and I reminded ourselves that this message of hope had been heard by many, in and out of prison. Some seeds need much germination. Who can tell how long it takes a man to turn what he has heard into treasure? I really felt a purpose now, that God had prepared me throughout my life to go and help others to find him and a purpose in their own lives.

Genesis 50:20 says: 'You intended to harm me, but God intended it all for good. He brought me to this position so I could save the lives of many people' (NLT). What a wonderful God we have! He can turn our mess into a wonderful message of hope, of love, and of joy, reconciliation and restitution.

14

Abundant Life

Knowing just how much emotion goes into each Kairos journey, I felt I needed a break. I knew that it was right for me to step away for a while, to pursue other avenues that God had for me.

I was still enjoying my working life. It was well paid, and I worked alongside some good people. I worked for a great company covering a lot of miles, all of which I enjoyed. The only hitch left in my life was getting special clearance in order to support technical issues in government institutions. It seemed impossible to get a permit with my record. Although successful with Kairos, I had failed other applications due to my past. Now, with fresh challenges ahead, I needed to find ways around it. There was nothing for it but to get down on my knees once again.

How I wished this record of my bad choices would stop following me around. But it seemed to me I had to get used to it, maybe for the rest of my life. I know there are always consequences for wrongdoing. But what about second chances too?

About that time, I discovered the company I worked for had a contract in the Falklands. Suddenly they were looking for an engineer to go out there for a four-month stint in order to service the agreement. Not only that, but there was also some serious money as part of the package. What an opportunity! I had been to the Falklands in the military and was very keen to go back. How could I make this a possibility on the back of so many security refusals?

Happily, around this time I was advised the official clearance department – the one necessary for issuing permits – had recently come under new jurisdiction. I was invited to reapply. I chalked this up as another godly intervention and – miracle of miracles – I was the proud owner of all the certification needed to clear the way not only to the Falklands, but also to other security premises as well. I knew all along the Falkland Islands had strict rules on drugs, but I had been honest in my application and somehow my road had been cleared.

It had all been a struggle. But true repentance – meaning turning your life around and facing in an opposite direction – will win in the end. Having that conviction of sin, which I did not have before and which comes from the Holy Spirit, led me to repent and to say sorry to God for the wrong things I had done and thought. This brought his forgiveness and restitution to my life.

The last hurdle, the manager's approval, also went well and I awaited the date for my leaving. It was tough leaving Suzanne and the children, but they were happy for me, knowing how much I wanted this experience.

My church was praying for me through the wait, equipping me for the spiritual work ahead. So too was Mike who, once again, through prayer, gave me a prophetic word. Having spent time together, Mike told me: 'Simon, you're not going solely for your company. You're going there to do the Lord's work.' I felt a tingle down my spine and prayed that was true.

The flight there was very long, sixteen hours with a stop-off at the Ascension Islands. I was exhausted when I finally arrived. However, the base at Mount Pleasant, which is essentially for military personnel, was very comfortable. I occupied an en suite room and ate in the sergeants' mess. But it didn't take me long to realize Mike's prediction had been spot on.

God had clearly gone before me and surrounded me with some wonderful Christians. Just after I arrived, Lisa, who was in the RAF, flew out and was a great Christian friend throughout my time there, along with another guy called Colin from St Helena, and also Trudi who lived in the Falklands. We had some great prayer times together.

It wasn't long after arrival that I paid my first visit to the base chapel. There I quickly became friendly with the RAF padre, Phil, who introduced me to other Christians living there. There were hardly any computers needing my service. I had plenty of time on my hands as I had very little work to do.

Together with Phil, I handed out a good number of 'Why Jesus?' leaflets. I also had an opportunity to give an account of my life at an Open Mic evening. I told them about myself, the prison work with Kairos and explained how the course was based around making good choices instead of bad ones. Afterwards, I felt the enemy attacking me for being so open with the audience. Later,

I found out that this could have got me off the island in a wink, as the event had taken place on a military base.

Phil and I also made trips to Port Stanley, the Falkland capital. I went to the cathedral a few times and then to the Tabernacle Church where I met Jackie, who was in charge. I made good friends with a couple who ran the local Mission to Seafarers, a charity my UK church also supports. That made it easy to forge an immediate connection.

More importantly, and for me more exciting, I discovered there was a prison in Port Stanley, and Phil and myself enquired if we could go and talk to the prisoners and share the gospel with them. Thanks to a lovely Christian prison officer, Brenda, this was arranged, and I was able to introduce myself and tell them my story. A few days later, one prisoner called us back. As a result of the visit, he had made a commitment to Jesus and wanted me to go and pray with him. What a privilege! I continued to pray for this man throughout my stay and after he was transferred to the UK.

There were other opportunities too, to pray with military personnel and civilians, all on the island for so many different reasons. The Falklands held such a distinctive mix of people, all drawn together in that snowy, barren land, which was in some ways so English and yet so very far from home.

Yes, I had been sent there to service technology and resolve technical issues. But there was so much more for me to do. That prophetic word had been so right. In addition to my main role, I knew I had been there to share

God's love and give encouragement alongside any technical expertise I could offer. It had broadened my horizons
and shown me new people lovingly committing to the
Christian message thousands of miles from home. How
my faith had deepened during those four months away
and how much I had learned.

Although I had enjoyed my stay, I was more than ready
to take the long flight home. I was excited about seeing
Suzanne and the children and telling my parents of my
adventures. I was even looking forward to going back to
my regular job. It was high time too, to thank my home
church for praying for me so faithfully. But bad news was
waiting for me.

My dad, John, had been ill on and off for many years
with emphysema as well as diabetes. During my time
away he had worsened and now needed constant oxygen
to help him breathe. He was finding it hard to walk at
all. A couple of months after I got home, Dad was rushed
into hospital where the doctors were concerned about his
chances of recovery. It was a big reality check.

However, an amazing thing happened a couple of days
before he was taken into hospital. I had begun juicing vegetables and was on a health kick. On this particular day I
had some fresh celery, along with some other vegetables,
that I juiced. Within fifteen minutes of drinking some
of it, I started to feel really ill; the sweat was pouring off
me and I had a really bad stomach ache. I lived near the
doctors' surgery and went down there. I was sick as I got
to the toilet in there. My face went completely red, and
my heart was beating fast. They took me immediately to

the doctor's room and called an ambulance. I was having anaphylactic shock. I went into atrial fibrillation and my heartbeat went up to 160 beats a minute.

I spent the day in hospital. It all calmed down and with the relevant drugs I recovered fully. The amazing thing was that this enabled me to have some days off work to spend with my dad.

Sadly, his condition worsened over the next few days. All the family was worried. But my biggest concern was wondering where Dad stood in relation to God. Even though our relationship had changed so much, I had no idea if he had a faith. I worried about his future and dearly wanted to know. It was time to call Mike.

'Can you come and pray for my dad?' I asked him.

Mike and Ann pencilled in a weekend date to come on a visit but, as I walked out of the ward, Mike phoned back. 'How about today?' he asked. Had he felt prompted? Or did he believe, like me, that some things simply can't wait?

Even though Dad had drifted in and out of consciousness, he seemed to recognize Mike and me straight away. Mike held his hand and immediately sensed that Dad's life was slipping away.

'Do you believe in God, John?' Mike asked.

'I do,' replied my dad, temporarily coming back to almost full consciousness. I waited. I had never got my dad to say anything about his beliefs. Now he wanted acceptance.

'Then let's say the Lord's Prayer together,' invited Mike, knowing that due to Dad's naval service, the words would not be new to him. Together, the three of us clearly repeated the familiar words with Dad now fully awake and aware. From somewhere, he had found the strength to ask forgiveness and speak those precious words in humility. Very soon afterwards, he slipped back peacefully into a coma.

Within hours, Dad had worsened. I had to collect Mum and rush back to the hospital, but we were too late. For me, there was deep sadness yet gratitude too. My dad had accepted God's gift of eternal life and I felt sure that we would meet again. It isn't the length of belief God counts, or any special words or actions. It's the sincerity of a person's changed heart that he values.

Dad and I had had a difficult relationship. All through my childhood there had been a burning resentment at his absences, his drinking, even his treatment of Mum. But God had dealt with all of that. God showed me very clearly that we are all products of our upbringing, so there was no blame anymore. I could not blame Dad any more than he could blame his father, or he could blame his father's father. We all have the ability through Jesus Christ to end the cycle, and after all we are all ultimately responsible for our own behaviour. There are no perfect parents. I always loved my dad; amidst the turmoil we had some wonderful times and he always provided for the family. Now that he was no longer around, I sensed his absence would leave a big hole.

It was a huge blow too, for my mum. After many turbulent years, she had to adjust to living alone again. Yet in her grief, I could sense her amazement at Dad's last-minute change of heart and declaration of faith. I could see it was stirring something deep within her. Mum and I had often spoken about the Christian life and, while patiently listening, she hadn't really understood. And that's despite seeing huge changes in my life. Now she had to deal with the reality of her larger-than-life, forceful, life partner, accepting that there was a God – One to whom we are all accountable. Until now, it had been a subject they had both politely ignored.

Now I knew Mum was missing out on the kind of comfort only God can give, at this time of bereavement. For the believer, there are sound words of consolation, promises from the Bible and the certainty of another life to help you through loss. When a Christian dies, there is a celebration to be had, knowing they are safely home. Sadness for those left behind, of course. But our home is not here, and partings are only temporary. And no matter how solitary it feels, we are never left alone. Ever.

I so wanted this for my mum. But I knew any immediate solution would have to be practical for her to accept it – put her with people, and believe God would do the rest. So I encouraged her to get out and volunteer somewhere where she felt useful and had good company around her. Happily, a new drop-in centre for the homeless had recently opened in the town, and they needed part-time kitchen staff. It fitted her like a glove.

Although nervous to start with, Mum soon settled in and had a great team to work with. She was impressed with the way other volunteers served the very poorest, and in total awe of the patience and understanding shown to those on the streets. She began to feel relaxed around such a caring team. New friendships were formed, a new world was opening up for her.

A little later, Mum started to accept invitations to come to church with the family each Sunday. To her surprise, she made new friends there too. Although she may have struggled a bit with the teaching – not always the easiest to fathom – she soon made her mark there, always the first to offer a helping hand. Then, at an Easter Day service, she took her own big step of faith. Through tears, she stood up and asked Jesus to be the Lord of her life. For my shy mum, that took the kind of courage I had first seen in prisoners when declaring God's touch on their lives. When asked how she felt, Mum simply answered: 'I can't escape the love that surrounds all you Christians.'

Later I had the privilege and joy of taking part in her baptism. It was a pivotal point in the life of the family. I was, at last, totally 'at one' with my parents. We would meet again – not in the stormy seas of this life but in the one to come. Through loss and new beginnings, through tears, anxiety and remorse, I was seeing yet again how God rescues and restores the years the locusts steal. I marvel again and again at his rescue of me. I could so easily have been blown up or shot at. Prison sentences might have been long and brutal, and addiction could have led to an early grave. And they would all have been my own choices. My very bad choices.

Another great moment for me was when my pastor, Graham, phoned Suzanne and me, and asked us to be on the leadership team of our church. What a transformation

God had performed on me: taking me out of a pit where my marriage was on the rocks, I was very low, almost suicidal and on drugs, to now leadership in the church and leading a Kairos week, and also becoming a trustee of the Kairos charity. God can and does transform lives if only we open ourselves up to him and let him in. Romans 12:2 is a very special verse that I cherish: 'Do not conform to the pattern of this world, but be transformed by the renewing of your mind. Then you will be able to test and approve what God's will is – his good, pleasing and perfect will' (NIV).

It has now been sixteen years since my deliverance in 2006 and the journey since has been amazing. Getting to know Jesus and being filled with the Holy Spirit is a wonderful experience. The joy that wells up from within me at times is indescribable and the peace from walking with Jesus and being in a family of Christians is such a contrast with what I knew before. This free gift is there for all of us. We can all have a relationship with Jesus because he died on the cross to set us free and rose again on the third day. He willingly sacrificed his life for us. What a wonderful gift! He conquered death and gave us the chance to have eternal life with him in heaven.

When I asked one man I spoke to in prison about Jesus, he replied 'I always knew Jesus was an important man, because he is the only one to have ever split time!' He meant that our whole date system is based on Jesus – before Christ (BC) and *anno Domini* (AD).

I am a work in progress; God is still healing me from past hurts and I still struggle at times, but I have my anchor and rock to hold onto. I incurred a lot of debt when I was taking drugs and gambling. I upped the mortgage many times to keep up with that lifestyle, but over time God has helped me get my finances back in order. I am not immune – and nor is any Christian – from human emotions. I still get angry and upset, tired, emotional and grumpy sometimes, but the difference now is that I can take them all to God and keep short accounts with him as he makes me more aware of them by his Holy Spirit.

I have also experienced the gift of healing from sinful traits that get handed down from our ancestors. My great-grandfather very sadly committed suicide by throwing himself off London Bridge due to gambling debts. When we come to know Jesus and give our lives to him, these generational curses can be cut and severed through prayer. With my history of gambling too, prayer certainly cured me of that.

Another great healing point for me was when the Lord showed me that I had been affected by a spirit of rejection that had come down the family line and was passed onto me by my father, probably around my time in Fiji. This may be why he had such trials and tribulations, as other spirits can manifest from the spirit of rejection, which would explain a lot of the issues we both experienced. There are many books on this subject and I would recommend that you seek guidance on this subject. Exodus 34:7 says: 'I lavish unfailing love to a thousand generations. I forgive iniquity, rebellion, and sin. But I do not excuse the guilty. I lay the sins of the parents upon their children and grandchildren; the entire family is affected – even children in the third and fourth generations' (NLT).

While this seems harsh and maybe not all Christians would agree on this point, I could certainly see this coming down my family line. But the wonderful thing is that when I fully accepted Jesus into my life, I was forgiven, redeemed and a restoration began in me.

It is amazing how the Lord can identify these issues in a person's life and how he can heal the wounds that so many of us carry, which can have a profound effect on how we act and make choices in our lives. This is how God transforms our lives and minds, puts us back into our true nature and gets us thinking straight again. The Lord can restore the years the locusts have stolen; this wonderful Scripture can be found in Joel 2:25.

I have happily met up with my elder son twice now and hopefully started a healing process whereby he will be able to forgive me. It is going to take time and may take many years, but with God's help all things are possible.

The older I get, the more accepting I am of my fallen human nature and really see my need for our Saviour and Lord Jesus Christ, who died for us on a cross to save us from our sins. You too can also accept this gift right now, if you say this prayer and believe in your heart. I can attest to the fact that Jesus Christ is real, and my prayer is that from my life and story, and from your own story, you will also see that he is real and accept the eternal life that is offered by believing in the risen Christ.

The Sinner's Prayer

Dear Lord Jesus, I know that I am a sinner and I ask for your forgiveness. I believe you died for my sins and rose from the dead. I turn from my sins and invite you to come into my heart and life. I want to trust and follow you as my Lord and Saviour.

It would be wrong to suggest that a Christian life is without its pitfalls. It isn't. We are all subject to the same fallen world we share with others. The difference is we have a wonderfully forgiving and loving God who will guide us through the good times as well as the hard times.

We are not made perfect in a flash. Neither is life without its awkward, life-changing options. It's not easy to get them right all the time, but we do have a handbook for life in the Bible. In Kairos we have an acronym for what the Bible means to us (Basic Instructions Before Leaving Earth) and we have the privilege of prayer to help us make the right choices – the sort of choices that please God even if, for us, it's incredibly uncomfortable.

In terms of years, I'm now well over halfway through my earthly life and have no idea what God has in store next. All I know for sure is that I'm loved by God – the Father who put a ring around a mine-field, made an Israeli judge smile rather than imprison me, and plucked me out of deadly addiction. And I didn't deserve any of it.

I merely share the truth of what I have discovered. There is nowhere too far, or sin too deep, that God can't reach it. Incredibly, all it takes is faith and a prayer.

I promise you it works.

If you would like to know more about Kairos prison ministry, you can find out here: www.kairosprisonministry.org.uk

Notes

1   This is how Val and I remember it, but I cannot find a verse in the Bible that exactly matches this. It may have been Joshua 1:9: 'Do not be afraid or discouraged. For the LORD your God is with you wherever you go' (NLT).

2   As noted, these were probably not the exact words, but it's how I remember it.

3   Neil T. Anderson, *The Bondage Breaker: Overcoming Negative Thoughts, Irrational Feelings and Habitual Sins* (USA: Monarch, 1993).

Authentic

We trust you enjoyed reading this book
from Authentic. If you want to be
informed of any new titles from this author
and other releases you can sign up to the
Authentic newsletter by scanning below:

Online:
authenticmedia.co.uk

Follow us: